CI

3

CI

A History of the Railways

By the same author:

The History of Flight (Heinemann)
Britain and the Modern World (Heinemann)
The Victorian Age (Heinemann)
The History of Transport in Britain:
    1700 to the present (Heinemann)
A History of the Motor Car (Pergamon)
A History of Britain, 1900–1939 (Pergamon)

A History of the Railways

by

JOHN RAY

Senior Master
The Hugh Christie School, Tonbridge

HEINEMANN EDUCATIONAL
BOOKS LTD · LONDON

Heinemann Educational Books Ltd
LONDON EDINBURGH MELBOURNE TORONTO
AUCKLAND SINGAPORE JOHANNESBURG
HONG KONG NAIROBI IBADAN

SBN 435 31754 7

Published by
Heinemann Educational Books Ltd
48 Charles Street, London W1X 8AH
Printed in Malta by
St Paul's Press Ltd, Malta

Contents

To Jane

Introduction

This book has been written especially for young people of secondary school age. It attempts to give an outline of the main developments in Britain's railway system and then to provide sufficient information for further research to be made. In modern education there is increasing use of the personal study. Many pupils show a great interest in discovering for themselves the details of a topic which they have chosen. A great number of these are undertaken for examination work.

The story of railways has much in it that appeals to young people. The pioneers showed determination and strong faith in their beliefs. Ingenuity was needed to overcome enormous obstacles. The dreams of the past have become the realities of the present.

The book has been written merely as a starting point. It makes no greater claim than that, but hopes to encourage and guide further research.

My thanks are due to Mr Paul Richardson of Heinemann Educational Books for his helpful, guiding friendship and to Miss Mary Mackintosh for her detailed care in collecting photographs. My family have very kindly enabled me to work un-hindered.

John Ray
Tonbridge, July, 1969

List of Illustrations

Acknowledgments

The author and publishers wish to thank the following for permission to reproduce copyright material:

The Science Museum: 2, 3, 4b, 5, 6, 7, 9, 10, 11, 12, 14, 15, 16, 18, 21, 24, 33, 56
British Railways Board: 1, 32, 36, 41, 42, 44, 45, 46, 59, 61, 62, 63
The Radio Times Hulton Picture Library: 8, 23, 25, 26, 34, 37, 52, 53
Keystone Press Agency Ltd: 40, 43, 64
Museum of British Transport: 17, 20, 31, 35, 38
Associated Press Ltd: 60
French National Railways: 47
London Transport Board: 51, 54, 55
Stephen Evans and the Festiniog Railway Company: 58
The Romney, Hythe and Dymchurch Railway Company: 57
Line's Bros Ltd and Triang Toys: 65
Railway Photo Service: 48
The Indian Railways Board: 49
The Mansell Collection: 22, 27, 28
Japanese Information Centre: 50
Imperial War Museum: 29, 30, 39

1. The Modern Scene

In the story of man's technical development Britain holds a proud place. Since the 18th century her inventors have helped to provide the world with a number of mechanical devices which have altered the style of people's lives. Progress has been made particularly in methods of transport. Today many people regularly make journeys in which they travel fast. By car, a pace of 40 m.p.h. is merely cruising. A train can easily cover the ground at 70 m.p.h. Aircraft often fly at speeds in excess of 500 m.p.h.

And yet for centuries man could not travel quickly. Journeys were made on foot, at an average speed of about 3 m.p.h. or on horseback at about 10 m.p.h. The major breakthrough in the search for a more rapid method of transport came in the early 19th century. Then the developing power of the steam engine was used to drive vehicles along iron rails. The railway was born. From that time the search for speed has been intensified. Faster vehicles have been designed and built. The modern world of rapid movement came into being.

In Britain the railways helped to change much of the country's economic and social life. They assisted people to travel widely and were used increasingly throughout the Victorian Age. The 19th century was their heyday. In the present century they have met with great competition, especially from the motor vehicle. Some Victorians thought of the railway as the limit of man's achievement in transport. They could not foresee any better method of land travel being devised. Yet today the railway system runs at a loss each year. Management and staff are searching for more efficient ways to organise the service.

As you are reading these words trains are speeding to many parts of Britain. Some are carrying heavy industrial goods from factory areas to the great seaports so that they can be sent for sale overseas. Others are express trains, travelling at high speed, taking passengers for business or pleasure on journeys of many miles. Many of Britain's large cities are only a few hours away from each other in time of travel. Other trains are transporting food or oil or cattle. Local services are taking workers or shoppers to their destinations. And all of this travel is taking place in relative safety. In fact, so many accidents occur in the home today that you are probably safer in a train than in your own house!

Although Britain's railways are experiencing difficulties at the present time, what will be their future? You will be alive in the 21st century. What changes will have occurred by then?

Some people believe that by the year 2000 the railway will hardly be used at all. Nearly all families will have their own form of road transport which will enable them to move with greater freedom than train travel can ever give. Railway tracks will be taken up and motorways will be built in their place, leading straight to the hearts of cities.

But others think that Britain will solve her transport problems only when she makes more use of her railways. High speed electric expresses will flash from England to Scotland or Wales at speeds of about 150 m.p.h. Monorails will be built to bring people from airports to nearby cities. Large freight-liner trains will carry goods quickly and efficiently.

To help you have a fuller appreciation of the problems of the present it is wise to see how they have arisen.

Fig. 1. A modern diesel express on the London-Edinburgh line.

2. The Steam Engine

One of man's greatest advances in modern times has been the way in which he has learned to produce and control power to do his work. At the present day it is possible to carry out gigantic schemes of building or providing energy because atomic energy and electricity, for example, have been controlled or power is produced from petrol engines. Where and when did all of this start?

A vast amount of modern technical progress can be traced back to the invention of the steam engine and its increasing use from the early years of the 18th century. Before that time, if man wished to carry out work, or travel about, there were four main methods of power available to him. These were man power, animal power, water or wind power. They had been used for centuries, but each had certain limits. Men and animals grew tired after some time and needed rest. Under certain weather conditions water-mills or windmills would not work. Can you suggest what these conditions were?

In the later part of the 17th century there was an increase of mining in Britain. Greater quantities of coal, copper and tin were needed. Therefore miners dug deep into the earth for them. As mines grew in depth they brought a new problem. This was the difficulty and danger of flooding. Labourers found that the workings were often flooded and sometimes it was impossible for them to carry on digging. A method of pumping the water away had to be found.

The answer to the problem was the introduction of steam pumps. They used the power produced by boiling water. You will have noticed this when a kettle boils. The lid is moved about by the force of the steam given off. If the steam were not allowed to escape, there would be an explosion. However, if it is controlled it can exert a considerable force.

Various experiments were made during the second half of the 17th century. They attempted to harness the power of steam and use it to drive an engine. Then the mines could be kept dry. Pumps could be worked day and night. Steam power does not tire; it does not depend upon certain weather conditions before it can work.

In 1698 Thomas Savery took out a patent for a pumping engine. Fig. 2 shows how it operated. It was advertised for use in mines but had a number of disadvantages. For example the pump could raise water only about thirty or forty feet. Therefore it became useless as soon as mining was carried on at greater depths.

A better engine was made by Thomas Newcomen. He was a Dartmouth ironmonger whose engines were first erected in the early years of the 18th century. A diagram of one is shown in Fig. 3. They were often built in engine houses and could pump up water from a considerable depth. Part of the machinery was a piston moving up and down inside a cylinder.

But Newcomen's pump, although employed widely in mines was rather inefficient. It used a large amount of fuel and much heat was wasted. Its size made it rather cumbersome.

In 1763 a model of one was given to James Watt who was working as an instrument maker at Glasgow University. Watt stands among the world's greatest inventors and was soon able to devise a method of retaining the engine's heat so that it could work more efficiently, using less fuel. His addition was called a condenser. The engine is shown in Fig. 4a.

To have his engines built Watt needed financial backing. He found this from Matthew Boulton who owned the Soho Iron Works, Birmingham. Their partnership was very successful and many of the new engines were sold in various parts of Britain and abroad. In 1781 Watt introduced an improvement with the double-acting steam engine, in which steam worked on both sides of the piston, thus increasing the power.

About the same time a most important step forward was taken in the development of the steam engine. This was the introduction of rotary motion. The engine could now turn a wheel and thus machinery could be driven. Fig. 4b shows how this worked. The possibilities were enormous because steam power was quite cheap and easy to produce in Britain.

Some factory owners began installing engines to drive the machines in their works. Far sighted inventors started experiments using steam power in transport. They reasoned that a wheel turned by

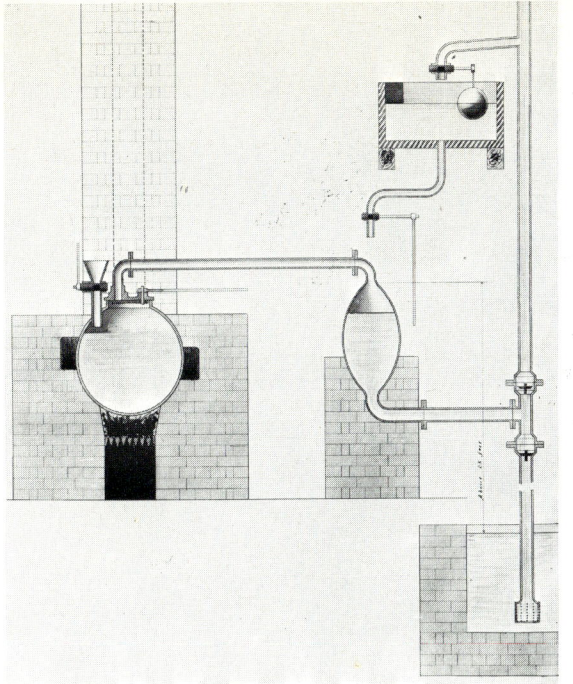

Fig. 2. The Savery engine.

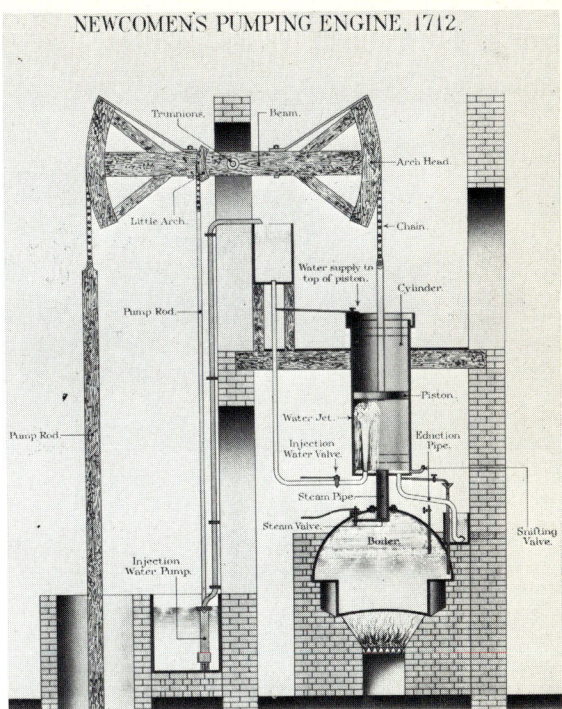

Fig. 3. The Newcomen engine.

steam could drive a ship through water or could move a vehicle on land.

The first steamship was built in 1798 and travelled at about 5 knots. By the early years of the 19th century ships were fitted with paddle wheels whose rotation drove the vessels along.

On land also, vehicles were designed to be driven by steam. In 1784 William Murdoch, who was employed at Boulton's Soho works, designed and built one. Other road vehicles were constructed by Richard Trevithick, a brilliant Cornish engineer. In 1803 he drove one of his engines in London, much to the amazement of passers-by.

But the greatest use of steam power was made during the 19th century on railways. The steam driven locomotive became a sign of Victorian progress and brought vast changes to everyday life. The next chapter will show how this new and revolutionary form of transport came into being.

Can you now find the answers to the following questions?

1. *What was an atmospheric engine?*
2. *Why was coal a very suitable fuel for producing steam power?*
3. *How could a rotary engine be used in a factory?*

Fig. 4a. The Watt engine.

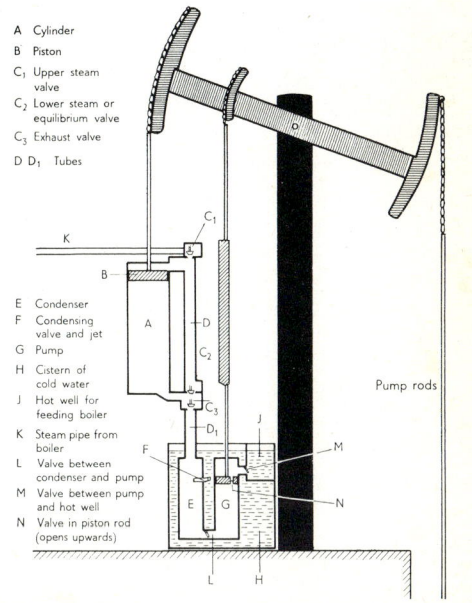

A Cylinder
B Piston
C_1 Upper steam valve
C_2 Lower steam or equilibrium valve
C_3 Exhaust valve
D D_1 Tubes

E Condenser
F Condensing valve and jet
G Pump
H Cistern of cold water
J Hot well for feeding boiler
K Steam pipe from boiler
L Valve between condenser and pump
M Valve between pump and hot well
N Valve in piston rod (opens upwards)

Fig. 4b. The Watt rotary engine.

3. Early Railways, before 1830

By the end of the 18th century a faster and more efficient form of transport was needed in Britain. The developments of the Industrial Revolution were leading to an increased production of goods and they had to be moved to areas where they could be bought. Coal and iron were two vital commodities in this new industrial age and it was necessary to move them about quickly in large quantities.

For many years before that time, trackways or waggonways had been used. Along them, trucks of coal were taken from the mines to nearby waterways. From there, cargoes were carried to towns and cities. Sometimes the trackways were deep ruts of hard packed earth. On other occasions wooden rails were laid and the trucks of coal were either pulled along them by horses or were manhandled. The wear on such rails was heavy and many replacements were needed. In the first half of the 18th century iron wheels were sometimes fitted to trucks and these wore out the trackways even more rapidly. Later, strips or plates of iron were nailed on to the wood in order to make it last

longer. This metal 'plateway' was the ancestor of of today's rails.

James Outram, who lived in the later part of the 18th century devised a plateway which used a flanged rail. A number of collieries bought and used lengths of his trackway. But his business partner, William Jessop, had a better idea. In 1789 he constructed a line which used 'edge rails'. Later they were set on wooden or stone sleepers and held by 'chairs'. Flanged wheels were fitted to the trucks. Good use was made of cast-iron, which, although rather brittle, was stronger than wood.

The combination of iron rails and steam vehicles led to the development of the railway system. After Trevithick's early experiments with road locomotives he turned his attention to vehicles which ran on rails. He was an engineer at the Pen-y-Darran Iron Works, Merthyr Tydfil, South Wales. There, in February 1804 one of his engines pulled a train loaded with 10 tons of iron and 70 men and showed some of the possibilities of this form of transport. But there were also problems. The cast-iron rails cracked under the weight. Later, in 1808,

Fig. 5. The Blenkinsop rack locomotive, 1812.

Fig. 6. Richard Trevithick.

Fig. 7. A wagonway for carrying coal, 1773

Trevithick brought his engine, *Catch-me-who-can* to London. It was used to give demonstrations, on a circular trackway, to the public for a small entry charge. But Trevithick did not continue his interest in railway locomotives and went to South America in 1816.

However, Trevithick did introduce one important feature to his engines. The exhaust steam was discharged into the chimney. Thus, instead of being allowed to escape wastefully, it helped to draw up the fire and make the engine more efficient.

One of the very first lines in Britain was the Surrey Iron Railway. It was constructed originally for the transport of chalk and corn from Croydon to London. Parliamentary permission had to be granted for the building of the line which was opened in 1803, but steam traction was not used. The trucks were pulled by horses along the railway or 'tramway'.

More attention was turned over the next few years to the improvement of locomotives. Some experiments were made with stationary engines. They were steam driven and were installed inside an engine house, often near to a mine. As the engine worked, cog-wheels turned large winding drums whose ropes were attached to trucks. Thus, loads could be drawn uphill.

In 1812, John Blenkinsop built a six-wheeled locomotive. The two middle wheels were cogged and the teeth fitted into notches arranged alongside one of the running rails. This 'rack' locomotive was intended to get a better grip on the rails as it moved along. It weighed 5 tons and cost about £400 to construct. Engines of this kind were used until about 1835 on a line which linked Middleton Colliery with Leeds.

Naturally the greatest interest in the possibilities of railways was shown in industrial areas. William Hedley was the engineer at Wylam Colliery. He did not believe that 'rack' wheels were needed and built the famous *Puffing Billy* in 1813. This engine had two vertical steam-jacketed cylinders, each with a diameter of 9 inches. The piston stroke was 36 inches, and drove the four wheels through a series of cogs. The engine worked for many years, accompanied later by *Wylam Dilly* which was also built for colliery work.

It was at this stage of the development of Britain's railways that there appeared one of the greatest names of transport history—George Stephenson.

Here are three questions for you to answer:

1. *What was a tramway?*
2. *What is the difference between a stationary engine and a locomotive?*
3. *What experiments did Trevithick carry out with steam driven road vehicles?*

4. George Stephenson

George Stephenson was born in 1781. His father was a labourer who earned his living as a colliery foreman. The family lived at Wylam, near Newcastle, in the area of Britain known as Tyneside. They were poor and at an early age George went out to work, having received no schooling.

By the time that he was 15 he became an assistant to his father, working with machinery. The boy realised that to make progress in life he needed to be educated. Therefore at the age of 18 he began to attend school in the evenings, after his work was finished. There he learned to read and write.

When he was 20 years old, George married. In time a son was born. He was named Robert and later joined with his father in carrying out some vast schemes of railway building. George Stephenson's wife died in 1806.

By 1812 he had shown such ability with engines that he was given the job of engineman at Killingworth Colliery. The wage paid was £100 per year, which was quite good at that time. George repaired machinery and built up the expert knowledge which he used later in dealing with engineering problems.

On one of his journeys back to Wylam, Stephenson saw Hedley's locomotive, *Puffing Billy*. He was very interested in its design and performance. Already he could foresee the possibilities of this new form of transport. Through his efforts, the owners of Killingworth Colliery were persuaded to use a locomotive at their pit. They asked Stephenson to design and build one. The result was the construction of the *Blücher*, which was named after the famous Prussian general.

There were technical difficulties. For example, the fuel did not burn very well. Like Trevithick before him, Stephenson thought of using the waste steam as a draught for the boiler fire. Thus the combustion would be improved. His ideas were introduced into his next engine, the *Killingworth No. 2* of 1815. Other improvements followed in the succeeding locomotives which he built.

In 1819 Stephenson was given the task of laying an 8-mile track from collieries at Hetton-le-Hole. This gave him practice in constructing a railway as well as building engines. His wisdom and experience were used in the work and his reputation grew.

Fig. 8. George Stephenson.

Fig. 9. The Rocket, *winner of the Rainhill trials.*

Fig. 10. The opening of the Stockton and Darlington Railway, 1825.

Soon after that time, Stephenson heard of an idea to build a railway from Stockton-on-Tees to Darlington. It had been discussed for several years and there was disagreement over whether a canal or a railroad would be better for transporting coal. There was an amount of opposition to a railway from people living in the district. A Bill seeking Parliamentary permission had been rejected in 1818. It was not passed until 1821.

A leading figure in the plan was Edward Pease, a wealthy man. One day, two visitors came to see him. One was George Stephenson, whom Pease liked immediately, later writing of him: 'There was such an honest, sensible look about George Stephenson, and he seemed so modest and unpretentious, and he spoke in the strong Northumberland dialect.'

The engineer persuaded Pease that steam locomotives should be used on the line and that passengers could be carried as well as freight. Stephenson was appointed to be engineer at a salary of £300 per year. He resurveyed the line thoroughly. It was opened on 27 September 1825.

First came a man on horseback carrying a red flag, then the 'Company's Locomotion Engine' driven by Stephenson. After the 'Engine's Tender' there were six waggons laden with coal and various goods. Then came many other waggons. One carried 'The Committee and other Proprietors in The Coach belonging to The Company'. The day was a triumphant success.

The line flourished and Timothy Hackworth was appointed to be engine superintendent. For many years he worked with George Stephenson who now turned his attentions towards a new venture. In the same year that the Stockton and Darlington Railway was opened a Bill was introduced to Parliament seeking permission to build a line from Liverpool to Manchester. It failed, but in 1826 a new route was planned and permission was obtained 'for making and maintaining a Railway or Tramroad from the town of Liverpool to the town of Manchester'. Trade was increasing rapidly in the area and the existing canal could not cater for all of it, therefore it was natural that the new railways were thought to be a possible means of transport. The directors had appointed George Stephenson as chief engineer and the formidable work began. Part of the difficult country to be crossed was Chat Moss where the railway had to float on a peat bog for four miles. Many people believed that men, rails and animals would all be swallowed up into the sphagnum moss, which was sometimes 20 or 30 feet deep. Stephenson used large hurdles, tree branches and hedge cuttings, to create a kind of large raft. Tar barrels were used as drain pipes. On this was placed gravel ballast and then the rails were laid. It was a very remarkable feat of engineering which often caused anxiety to the promoters of the railway, but proved itself in practice.

Other difficulties existed. Cuttings had to be made, tunnels dug, viaducts constructed and 63 bridges built. But before the line had been completed, an important matter came up for consideration. What type of locomotion should be used? Some favoured stationary engines with ropes attached. Others, including Stephenson wanted to employ locomotives. Therefore the company decided to offer a prize of £500 for the best locomotive which could meet their requirements.

Certain conditions were laid down. For example, each locomotive had to haul a load at least three times its own weight at more than 10 m.p.h. The boiler pressure was not to exceed 50 lb. per square inch. The trials were to take place at Rainhill, near Manchester.

There were four entries. They were the *Novelty*, entered by Braithwaite and Ericson, the *Sanspareil* by Hackworth, the *Perseverance* by Burstall and the *Rocket* by George Stephenson. The two most promising engines were the *Sanspareil* and the *Rocket*.

The trials covered a number of days and they proved the superiority of the *Rocket* over its competitors. The locomotive had been designed by George Stephenson and built by his son, Robert, at their Newcastle works. The latter had managed the works since 1827. Two notable features of the engine were, first its use of steam to generate a draught for the boiler and second, its use of 25 copper tubes, each 3 inches in diameter to convey the heat of the firebox thus increasing efficiency.

The *Rocket* pulled a load of $12\frac{3}{4}$ tons at an average speed of 13.8 m.p.h. and on another occasion raced along at almost 30 m.p.h. The handsome prize was won comfortably.

The opening day of the Liverpool and Manchester Railway was set for 15 September 1830. Eight engines took part in the various ceremonies which marked the historic event. The Prime Minister, the famous Duke of Wellington was present. Unfortunately, the day was marred by an accident to a Member of Parliament, William Huskisson:

> The duke advanced to meet him, and the two statesmen heartily shook hands. Then a melancholy catastrophe ensued. There appears to have been a little confusion caused by the approach of one of the engines; and Mr Huskisson, in his haste to get into a car, fell on the line. He was enabled to move a little out of the engine's track, or it would have gone completely over his head and breast. In the position he occupied, it went over his left leg, breaking it in two places . . .[1]

Huskisson died as a result of the accident, but the railway was a great success, carrying goods and passengers in large numbers. Once it was shown that a railway could be run at a profit, lines were started in various other parts of Britain.

George Stephenson, the 'Father of English Railways' lived on till 1848, by which time there were thousands of miles of working lines in existence. Much is owed to him, not only for his shrewd commonsense in engine construction and civil engineering but also for his vision of what transport could achieve:

> Burghley, January 28th, 1834 . . . Stephenson, the great engineer, told Lichfield that he had travelled on the Manchester and Liverpool railroad for many miles at the rate of a mile a minute . . . and that he had ascertained that 400 miles an hour was the extreme velocity which the the human frame could endure, at which it could move and exist.[2]

Now for some questions:
1. *What was the job of an enginewright at a colliery?*
2. *Why did railways begin in colliery areas?*
3. *What work today is carried out by a civil engineer?*

[1] *A History of England*, Hume and Stafford
[2] The Greville Memoirs

5. The Railway Boom, 1830–1850

In the twenty years after 1830 there was an enormous amount of railway building all over Great Britain. The new method of transport was shown to be fast, reaching speeds that had previously been thought impossible or dangerous. Goods and passengers could be carried in large quantities. Canals and roads, which were the main competitors of the railways, suffered a reduction in their traffic. By canal, goods travelled at the plodding pace of the horse on the towpath. On the roads, an average of 15 m.p.h. achieved by a coach was slow compared with the 35–40 m.p.h. of the train. Therefore the railway was well suited to the needs of Britain's Industrial Revolution.

Of course, there was opposition from certain people. Some believed that danger lurked in 'the new fangled devices'. A writer commented:

> What can be more palpably absurd and ridiculous than the prospect held out of locomotives travelling twice as fast as stage coaches! We should as soon expect the people of Woolwich to suffer themselves to be fired off upon one of Congreve's ricochet rockets as trust themselves to the mercy of a machine going at such a rate. We will back old Father Thames against the Woolwich Railway for any sum. We trust that Parliament will, in all railways it may sanction, limit the speed to eight or nine miles an hour, which we entirely agree with Mr Sylvester is as great as can be ventured on with safety.[1]

Even some who had experienced a ride on a train could still be terrified:

> The quickest motion is to me frightful, it is really flying, and it is impossible to divest yourself of the notion of instant death to all, upon the least accident happening. It gave me a headache which has not left me yet ... The smoke is very inconsiderable indeed, but sparks of fire are abroad in some quantity.[2]

Landowners often disliked the coming of the 'iron horse' to estates where life changed slowly. Sir Astley Cooper, surgeon to George IV wrote to Robert Stephenson of his fears:

> You are proposing to cut up our estates in all directions for the purpose of making an un-necessary road ... If this sort of thing be permitted to go on, you will in a very few years destroy the nobility.[3]

In spite of all opposition the building went on. In the north of England many small lines were built to link iron works to collieries or factory areas with seaports. Examples were the Durham Junction Railway and the Cromford and High Peak Railway. A remarkable line of the time was built in Kent, where the Canterbury and Whitstable Railway linked the cathedral city with a small port. An early line in the capital was the London and Greenwich Railway which was complete by 1838.

Gradually the pioneer builders lengthened the lines. Large centres some distance apart from each other were linked by rapid services. By 1837 the Grand Junction Railway joined Liverpool and Manchester with Birmingham. Then Robert Stephenson showed his enormous abilities by building the London and Birmingham Railway. It was one of the greatest feats of civil engineering carried out during the 19th century. At Tring in Hertfordshire a cutting had to be made for some two miles through the chalk. At Kilsby in Northamptonshire, a tunnel one and a half miles in length cost a number of lives and months of time to construct. But by 1838 a passenger could travel by train from Euston Station, with its imposing front, through Birmingham and on to Liverpool. From that port ships left on the voyage to America.

Another seaport which was connected with the Atlantic trade was Bristol. Soon, businessmen there wanted the railway to link them with the capital. An engineer was appointed. He was the brilliant Isambard Kingdom Brunel, who planned a route. It ran through country where the gradients were comparatively easy so that good speeds could be achieved. There were some fine feats of engineering. The Brent Valley was crossed by a viaduct 960 feet long which cost £40,000. The Box Tunnel presented great difficulties and was said to have cost £100 for every yard advanced.

Brunel's work was remarkable for his belief in

[1] *Quarterly Review*, March 1825
[2] Thomas Creevey
[3] Sir Astley Cooper to Robert Stephenson

Fig. 11. A train in the 1840's running on wooden rails.

Fig. 12. George Hudson, the Railway King.

Fig. 13. Railways in 1844.

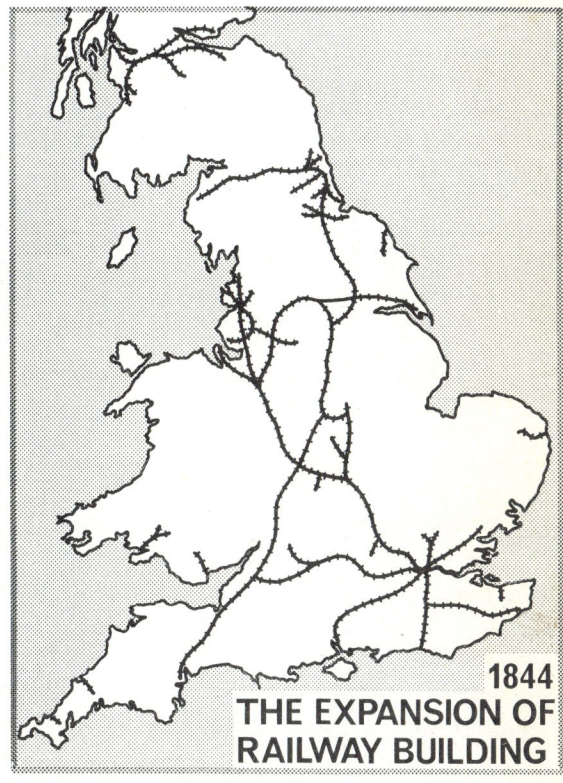

1844
THE EXPANSION OF
RAILWAY BUILDING

the broad gauge. This was 7ft 0¼in. In his view it was the best for railways, allowing speed to be combined with safety. The drawback was that other railways used a narrower gauge and therefore the Great Western stood alone. Parliament decided this in 1846 when 4ft 8½ins became standard gauge. With his usual good sense, George Stephenson had previously commented on gauge:

> I tell you the Stockton & Darlington, the Liverpool & Manchester, the Canterbury & Whitstable, and the Leicester & Swannington must all be 4ft 8½ins. Make them of the same width; though they may be a long way apart now, depend upon it they will be joined together some day.[1]

The planning and building of railways became an exciting and large scale business during the 1840's. Lines were constructed in many parts of the British Isles, sometimes opening up areas where life had hardly changed for centuries. Often the lines were small, originating in the enthusiasm of a a few local businessmen. At the time, the State did not have the power which it possesses today. There was a strong belief in freedom and competition in business. Therefore scores of small companies laid down railways, sometimes rivalling each other by having two separate lines to one town. Can you find the name of any place where this was done? The State interfered as little as possible, although it had to pass some measures, for example, to ensure the safety of passengers.

In the years 1845–1846 there was a 'Railway Mania' when many new lines were built and others were amalgamated, that is, joined together for more efficient running. There were thousands of pounds to be made from this. Fortunes were made and lost by investors who saw the railway as a highly profitable business concern. Sometimes there was fraud. The best known case was that of George Hudson, the 'Railway King', who launched many schemes which proved eventually to be unsound. Many people were left with shares that were worthless.

By 1850 there were more than 6000 miles of railway line in Great Britain. Mail, industrial goods and passengers were carried at speed by a system of transport that was envied in many parts of the World. The nation benefited; trade was made easier. When the Great Exhibition was held in London during 1851 many of the 6 million who attended came by train. The Queen herself had used the new means of travel, as the following newspaper account of 1840 shows:

> The Great Western Railway Company, anticipating the Patronage of the Queen and her illustrious Consort, Prince Albert, and of the Members of the Royal Family, have just had built a splendid royal carriage for their accommodation . . . The saloon is handsomely arranged with hanging sofas of carved wood in the rich style of Louis XIV, and the walls are panelled out in the same elegant manner, and fitted up with crimson and white silk . . .[2]

Can you answer these questions?
1. *Of the objections put forward to early railways, which were sound?*
2. *Was the broad gauge generally safer than the standard gauge?*
3. *When was the Royal Mail first carried by train?*

[1] George Stephenson
[2] The Hon. Alexander Gordon, 1850

Fig. 14. Navvies building a retaining wall at Camden Town in North London, 1838.

6. The Navvies

Excavations of motorways or building sites today are carried out with the aid of many mechanical devices. Electric power is used. Bulldozers, earth dumpers, concrete mixers and lorries are widely employed. The modern workman can rely on many methods of power to help his own efforts.

It is remarkable that the early railways were constructed, to a great extent by men alone, without any modern mechanical marvels. Sometimes as you make a railway journey, the route rides high along an embankment or cuts deep for perhaps half a mile through a cutting. It is more than likely that they were formed by large gangs of men using picks and shovels to excavate the thousands of tons of earth which had to be moved. It was then usually loaded into waggons or carts which were drawn by horses and carted away to be dumped. If solid rock stood in the way of progress, gunpowder was often used to blast a way through, then the work gangs moved in for the slow, laborious business of clearing away the debris.

The men who did the hard physical work of building Britain's railways were called 'navvies'. In the 18th century such men had been employed to construct canals, or 'navigations' and therefore they were referred to as 'navigators'. The busy Victorian Age, buzzing with industrial activity, gave much employment to thousands of men who had usually received no education but were strong in body. They had to be prepared to work long hours, often in conditions of the greatest danger, for their wages, which could be 5s a day, but were often less. For example, of the workmen involved in building the London and Birmingham Railway:

> By the current standards the navvies were paid well. But they had to work up to sixteen hours for their two or three shillings a day, and their lodgings and food were deplorable.[1]

Some of the construction workers were local men who were hired by the contractor to work for the period of time that the railway was being built through their district. When that section was finished they would return to some other form of employment. But there were also the professional navvies who travelled about the country, hiring themselves out to railway builders. They were a strange, fierce race:

> The navvy was the aristocrat, the expert ... He was paid twice as much as the labourer, and he emphasised his superiority by the colourful clothing he habitually wore. The labourers did the ordinary digging and hewing, mostly in their own districts, while the gangs of navvies were imported for the more difficult and dangerous parts of the work.[2]

[1] From 'The London and Birmingham' by R. Hough, in *History Today*, Aug. 1951
[2] *Railwaymen's Gallery*, R. Lloyd

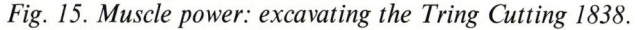

Fig. 15. Muscle power: excavating the Tring Cutting 1838.

Local people feared them and their behaviour sometimes led to strong opposition being aroused against the bringing of the railway to certain areas. On Saturday night, when they had been paid, they left the camps in which they lived to drink heavily in the nearby towns, sometimes quarrelling noisily and violently with each other and with the local inhabitants. But the navvy had a great pride in himself and his work, and often showed strong loyalty to his employer. Commenting on them in 1851, one writer said:

> Rude, rugged and uncultivated, possessed of great animal strength, collected in large numbers, living and working entirely together they are a class and community to themselves... They lived but for the present; they cared not for the past; they were indifferent to the future. They were a wandering people, who only spoke of God to wonder why he had made some so rich and others so poor.[1]

The employers of these labourers were the famous civil engineers of the 19th century. Lacking mechanical aids they appointed agents to take on a massive labour force. It has been estimated that in 1846 there were some 200,000 navvies. They worked for such men as Thomas Brassey and William Cubitt who faced and successfully solved the enormous problems of construction which the railways brought.

The dangers of their work led to a high rate of casualties. There were no inspectors to safeguard standards. Many navvies showed little respect for life and limb. They had a hard job to do and were comparatively well paid for it, therefore they drove on relentlessly, even when disaster came:

> Work on the tunnels and on the embankments and cuttings was dangerous and life was cheap. The tunnel miners drew extra pay, but their high casualty rate caused an outcry even in those conscienceless days. In Watford tunnel ten men were buried when one of the shafts collapsed. It took three weeks to dig out their bodies, to the delight of the local traders who set up refreshment booths and made a small fortune from the spectators.[2]

Much of Britain's vast railway network was built by these men, working under bad conditions. As the century progressed and developments were made with such tools as mechanical diggers and steam hammers, they were no longer needed. Some settled in a district where they had worked, others found employment on the railways which they had helped to create. But others were restless and travelled to many parts of the world, building railways in foreign lands which wished to copy Britain's new system of transport.

The following questions are about navvies:
1. *What was the origin of the name 'navvies'?*
2. *How many mechanical aids can you name which are used by modern contractors?*

[1] Source unknown
[2] From 'The London and Birmingham' by R. Hough, in *History Today*, Aug. 1951

Fig. 16. Rail chairs and keys: the Midland Railway, 1850.

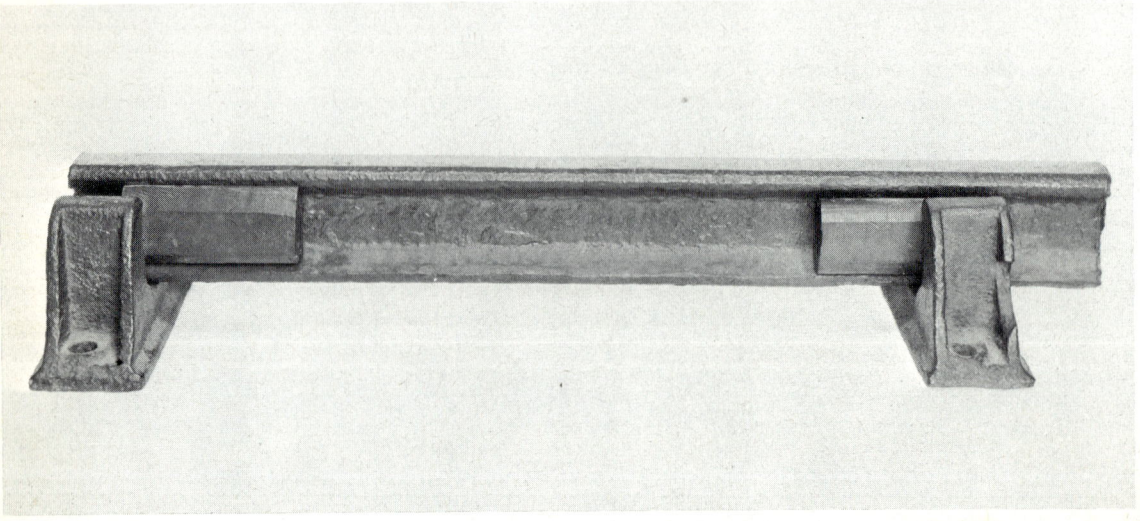

7. Some Aspects of Railways, to 1850

This chapter deals with various aspects of railways before 1850.

Carriages

The first railway carriage which was designed for carrying passengers was the 'Experiment'. It was used on the Stockton and Darlington Railway in 1825. The carriage resembled a stage coach. The passengers inside sat facing each other during journeys which could not have been very comfortable. The underframe had no springs and was supported by cast-iron wheels. The 'Experiment' had a deal table inside on which candles were placed when it grew dark.

Many early carriages were built in imitation of stage coaches. They were used by First Class passengers. Sometimes their own private carriages were carried on trucks at 6d per mile, the occupants paying an additional 2d per mile. Usually the First Class fare was 3d per mile.

The Second Class passengers travelled in plainer coaches, with less comfort. There was less padding on the seats, although there was, at least, a roof as protection against the weather.

The earliest Third Class coaches did not have this. They were trucks, often fitted with hard benches, but sometimes having no seats, only a handrail on which to cling. One of the first improvements made by the Manchester and Leeds Railway which opened in 1841 was to bore holes in the floor to let the rain out!

By 1850 railway companies began to realise that to encourage passengers to use their lines greater comfort had to be provided.

Locomotives

Throughout this period, improvements were made in the design and performances of locomotives. The early ones had four wheels, but it was found that they tended to 'pitch' at speed. Therefore longer engines with six wheels were built. They could pull greater loads.

Alterations were made to slide valves controlling the steam entering the cylinders, so that fuel was used economically. Engine boilers were length-ened to make greater use of fire tubes. The 'link motion' valve gear was invented in 1841.

Among the engines of the time there were 'singles' which employed one pair of large driving wheels, often more than 7 feet in diameter. A famous one was the *North Star*, built for the Great Western Railway in 1837.

The famous locomotive engineers included such names as Robert Stephenson, I. K. Brunel and Daniel Gooch.

Rails

Railway lines were constructed of wrought iron rails which were laid on wooden sleepers. They were held in iron 'chairs', fixed to the sleepers. The need for rails helped the iron industry to expand its production. However, by 1850 the heavier weights of trains and their increased speeds pointed the way to the need for steel in production.

The 'Battle of the Gauges' was lost by Brunel. Gradually the standard gauge of 4ft 8½ins was adopted and even the G.W.R. had to give way in 1892 and adopt that measurement.

Railway Clearing House

This organisation was set up in 1842. Often goods and passengers travelled on a journey which took them over the lines of several companies. For convenience, a through ticket was bought. The question then arose of how much of the fare or freight charge should be given to each company. The job of the Railway Clearing House was to share out the money. The receipts in the first year of operation were £193,246.

Signalling

From the earliest days the movement of trains has had to be carefully controlled. A train weighing over a hundred tons and travelling at 30 m.p.h. could cause enormous damage to life and materials if not properly checked. Therefore, signalling systems were soon developed.

At first, men known as 'policemen' were posted at intervals to signal with flags or lamps. An interval

Fig. 17. The North Star*, a broad gauge locomotive.*

of time had to elapse between trains to ensure that there were no crashes. Later a 'block system' was devised to keep a safe distance between two trains.

Signals were used from 1834. Some could be seen and worked like semaphore arms by day, or coloured lights by night. The Cooke and Wheatstone electric telegraph enabled messages to be sent between signal boxes or stations to ensure the safety of travel. This became an important principle in the British railway life.

Speed

One advantage of the railway over any other form of transport was its speed. The *Rocket* soon achieved 30 m.p.h. By the 1840's passenger trains were travelling comfortably at 45–50 m.p.h. In 1846, Gooch's engine, the *Great Western*, reached a speed of almost 60 m.p.h. while pulling a 100-ton load between Swindon and London. Such speeds altered a great deal of everyday life in Britain.

Staff

In the early days, drivers and firemen, both of whom had specialised jobs, were in short supply. Many had to be trained in the new skills. Others had gained experience in the engine houses of northern coal mines.

Signalmen, guards and clerical staff were often recruited from the areas where the lines had been built.

Each company developed its own uniform for staff and they were expected to show a smart appearance while on duty.

In 1845 an engine driver could earn more than £2 per week, while a general labourer received less than £1.

Tickets

The earliest railway tickets were made from paper. A clerk wrote on them such details as the passenger's name and the destination of the journey. It was a slow business.

In 1832 the Leicester and Swannington Railway introduced small brass tablets for the third-class passengers. The tablets were collected by the guard during the journey and then taken back to the station of issue.

16

Fig. 18. Euston Station, 1837; note the unroofed third class carriages.

Thomas Edmondson became a station master on the Newcastle and Carlisle Railway in 1836 and he introduced the idea of cardboard tickets which were stamped with the date. He was the pioneer of the modern system of preparing and selling tickets.

Season tickets were soon in use. At first they were called 'periodical tickets'.

Timetables

In the interests of safety and for the convenience of passengers, trains had to run to a regular timetable. During the early days railway companies advertised their services in local newspapers or on station boards. Later they brought out printed sheets and pamphlets containing the information.

The most famous railway timetable was *Bradshaw's Guide* which was published from 1839. It was a complete list of all companies' train services, contained in a single book.

Victorian stations

When railways were new in Britain many of the stations were built of wood, especially in country areas. Later, bricks and iron girders were used in the style of architecture which can still be seen at a number of stations. The high arched roof at a terminus was to allow the escape of steam from locomotives which were standing at the platform.

Gradually, greater comfort was provided for passengers in the form of waiting rooms on the platforms.

Try to answer the following questions without looking back at the chapter that you have just read:
1. *What was the name of the first railway carriage designed for carrying passengers?*
2. *Name a disadvantage of four wheeled locomotives.*
3. *When was the Railway Clearing House set up?*
4. *Who were the 'policemen' on railways?*
5. *What was a* Bradshaw?

8. Expansion, 1850–1914

By 1850 the railway had become a new and popular method of transport for the inhabitants of Great Britain. Between that year and the outbreak of the First World War in 1914 many more miles of track were laid. They stretched out to remote areas of England, Ireland, Scotland and Wales. Soon it was possible to travel from one end of the country to the other. In 1853 there were about 7000 miles of line. This number had increased to 13,500 miles by 1870 and 17,700 miles in 1893. At the end of this period more than 20,000 miles of railway had been laid down. The railway had been one of the great wonders of the Victorian Age.

There were more amalgamations. Often, larger companies took over the lines of smaller ones, thus producing some giant networks. For example, the North Eastern Railway was formed in 1854 from the York and North Midland, and the York, Newcastle and Berwick. The Great Eastern Railway was founded in 1862. By 1914 there were many companies in existence but the larger concerns had control of most lines.

The 19th century witnessed a remarkable increase in the use of iron. British industries connected with iron benefited greatly from railway building. The metal was needed for such things as engines, coaches, signals and rails. Cast iron and wrought iron, however, could not stand heavy and constant wear. Therefore before the 1850's sections of track often had to be replaced. With the coming of cheap steel, especially after the invention of the Bessemer Converter in 1856, there was an improvement. It is said that some steel rails laid at Derby in 1857 remained there for sixteen years, whereas the wrought iron track previously used had been changed four times a year. The weight of rails was about 80 lb. to 100 lb. per yard.

As railway companies settled to their work and began to gather experience they improved their rolling stock. Locomotives were made more efficient. They were built larger and compound steam engines brought more driving power. Speeds increased as companies competed to encourage passengers to use their lines. Some wonderful feats of driving were seen in those years. For example, in 1895 races were held to see whether the route to Aberdeen was faster by the east or the west coast route.

More comfort was given to passengers although travel could still be adventurous as the following 'Rules for Railway Travelling' of 1859 show:

> Rule 2—Never sit in any unusual place or posture. On some lines of railway seats are provided on the roofs of the carriages. These are to be avoided ... If a second-class carriage, as sometimes happens, has no door, (passengers) should take care not to put out their leg.

> Rule 9—Beware of yielding to the sudden impulse to spring from the carriage to recover your hat which has blown off, or a parcel dropped.[1]

Conditions improved. From 1873 the Midland

Fig. 19. Railways in 1852.

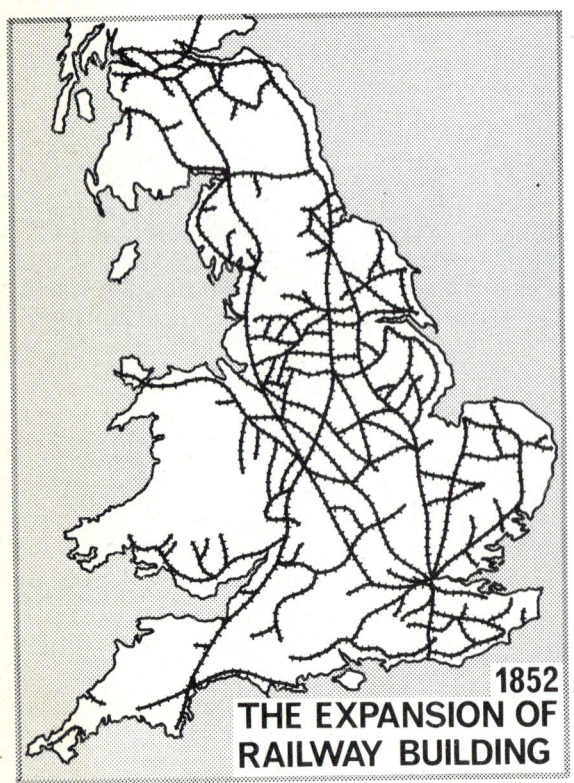

1852
THE EXPANSION OF
RAILWAY BUILDING

[1] *Rules for Railway Travelling*, 1859

Fig. 20. (above) Paddington Station in the 1850's.   *Fig. 21. (below) Railway staff in the 1860's.*

Fig. 22. An express corridor train at speed, 1897.

Railway decided to have upholstered seats for all compartments, including those of the Third Class. Passengers had not always been so well treated. Commenting on railway travel in the 1850's a Frenchman wrote:

> They even take off the third-class carriages and sometimes the seconds also, so as to oblige one to travel first. The cheapest seats are mostly uncovered, and in a country where it rains perpetually can one imagine anything more barbarous? The second-class compartments have wooden benches and back rests, no upholstering of any kind. The windows are unglazed and only provided with wooden shutters.[1]

Sleeping cars and Pullman cars were also built at that time and made travel very comfortable.

As the mileage of lines increased, certain towns became famous as railway centres. Sometimes they lay at the junctions of important routes. On other occasions they developed as centres for building rolling stock or as collecting points for goods wagons. Among them were Swindon, Wolverhampton and Crewe.

By 1914 the railway had brought many changes to the economic and social life of Great Britain. It had become a major means of transport and was far faster than any other. Canal companies whose barges made a steady but slow progress could not compete. Travel by road declined. Stage coaches were far less comfortable than trains, as well as being slower. Coaching inns lost their trade. Railway travel was comparatively cheap at 1d or 2d per mile and people flocked to take advantage of it.

The railways also provided employment for thousands of men. They were needed for all types of work connected with ensuring that the system ran efficiently. Track had to be laid and maintained, trains driven and cleaned, tickets sold and collected.

The country's economic life benefited because goods could be transported quickly and easily. Produce went rapidly from farms to cities; manufactured articles were sent at speed from factories to shops.

People of all classes travelled far more than at any previous time of history. In 1884, Sir James Allport said:

> When the poor man travels, he has not only to pay his fare, but to sink his capital, for his time is his capital; and if he now consumes only five hours instead of ten in making a journey, he has saved five hours of time for useful labour—useful to himself, his family, and to society.[2]

Some made journeys for the first time in their lives, perhaps on an excursion organised by Mr Thomas Cook. As railways were built to coastal towns, some developed as holiday centres for example, Blackpool in the north and Margate in the south.

By the outbreak of the First World War Britain had a vast network of railway tracks. Each company had its own colours for stock and uniform for staff. A large part of the nation's life depended upon steam powered transport.

Now try to answer the following questions:

1. *How many miles of railway track were there in Britain by 1914?*
2. *Name two advantages of iron over steel in railway construction.*
3. *Name two famous railway towns.*
4. *What effects did the railways have on other forms of transport?*

[1] From *A Frenchman sees the English in the Fifties*, adapted from the French of Francis Wey by Valerie Pirie
[2] Sir James Allport, 1884

9. Some Aspects of Railways, 1850–1914

The following chapter deals with various aspects of railway development between 1850 and 1914.

Brakes

The first brakes used for stopping trains were adapted from those found on horse-drawn carriages. A block was applied to the wheel by moving a hand lever. Such a brake was quite inefficient, however. A heavy iron locomotive moving at 30 m.p.h. needed a stronger means of halting its momentum. Therefore a type of hand brake was fitted which replaced the lever by a screw and a nut. By turning a handle the fireman was able to bring gradual but steady pressure to the brakes. Yet even this system was not particularly efficient. A driver of a train in the 1860's, pulling nine or ten small four-wheeled carriages would have to begin braking about two miles before the station at which he wished to stop, if he were travelling at speed.

Later a steam brake was used to operate on the locomotive's wheels, being regulated by the driver. But even this had disadvantages as the weights and speeds of trains increased. Sometimes, when the brakes were applied, the engine would continue to slide along with all of the wheels locked. What was needed was a method of applying brakes to all the wheels of the train.

The best answer was the compressed air-brake invented by an American, George Westinghouse in 1869 and improved three years later. Compressed air was used to operate the brakes under each carriage for the whole length of the train. Thus travel was made safer.

Carriages

Throughout the period more attention was paid to providing comfort for passengers. On the early railways, carriages had been lit by oil lamps, which were not very efficient. Later, incandescent gas lighting was used. By 1914 electricity was coming into wider use and this form of illumination was employed on some trains.

Carriages grew in length and width. From four-wheelers they increased to six-wheelers. Later, eight-wheelers, mounted on sprung bogies were designed and they added to the comfort of passengers. Early carriages had consisted of separate compartments. From the 1880's corridors were introduced to allow travellers to move along the train.

Dining cars, mainly introduced in the 1890's enabled passengers to take meals when making long journeys.

Comfort within compartments improved, with elaborate upholstery and fittings. Before steam heating was introduced passengers would sometimes be provided with foot warmers for winter journeys.

Carriages were usually made of wood, teak being widely used because of its strength. Later metal was employed to give greater strength.

Companies

A large number of amalgamations took place in these years, yet by 1914 there were still a large number of railway companies. Each one worked on the capital, or money invested by shareholders. They expected to receive interest each year on their investments. Some lines prospered better than others and had a higher reputation for efficiency. In 1914 the Midland Railway had the largest capital and the biggest stock of trucks and carriages. The Great Western Railway had most track. The Great Eastern Railway carried most passengers.

Here is a list of Britain's main companies at that time:

1. The Great Western
2. The Great Southern & Western
3. The London & South Western
4. The South Eastern & Chatham
5. The London, Brighton & South Coast
6. The Midland
7. The Great Central
8. The Great Eastern
9. The Lancashire & Yorkshire
10. The North Eastern
11. The Great Northern
12. The London & North Western
13. The Highland
14. The North British
15. The Great North of Scotland
16. The Glasgow & South Western
17. The Caledonian

Fig. 23. *New saloon carriage on the London, Brighton & South-Coast Railway, 1873.*

Fig. 25. *(right) Scenes from a Pullman Palace Carriage on the Midland Railway, 1874.*

Fig. 24. *A 0-6-0 goods locomotive of the L.N.W.R. in the 1860's.*

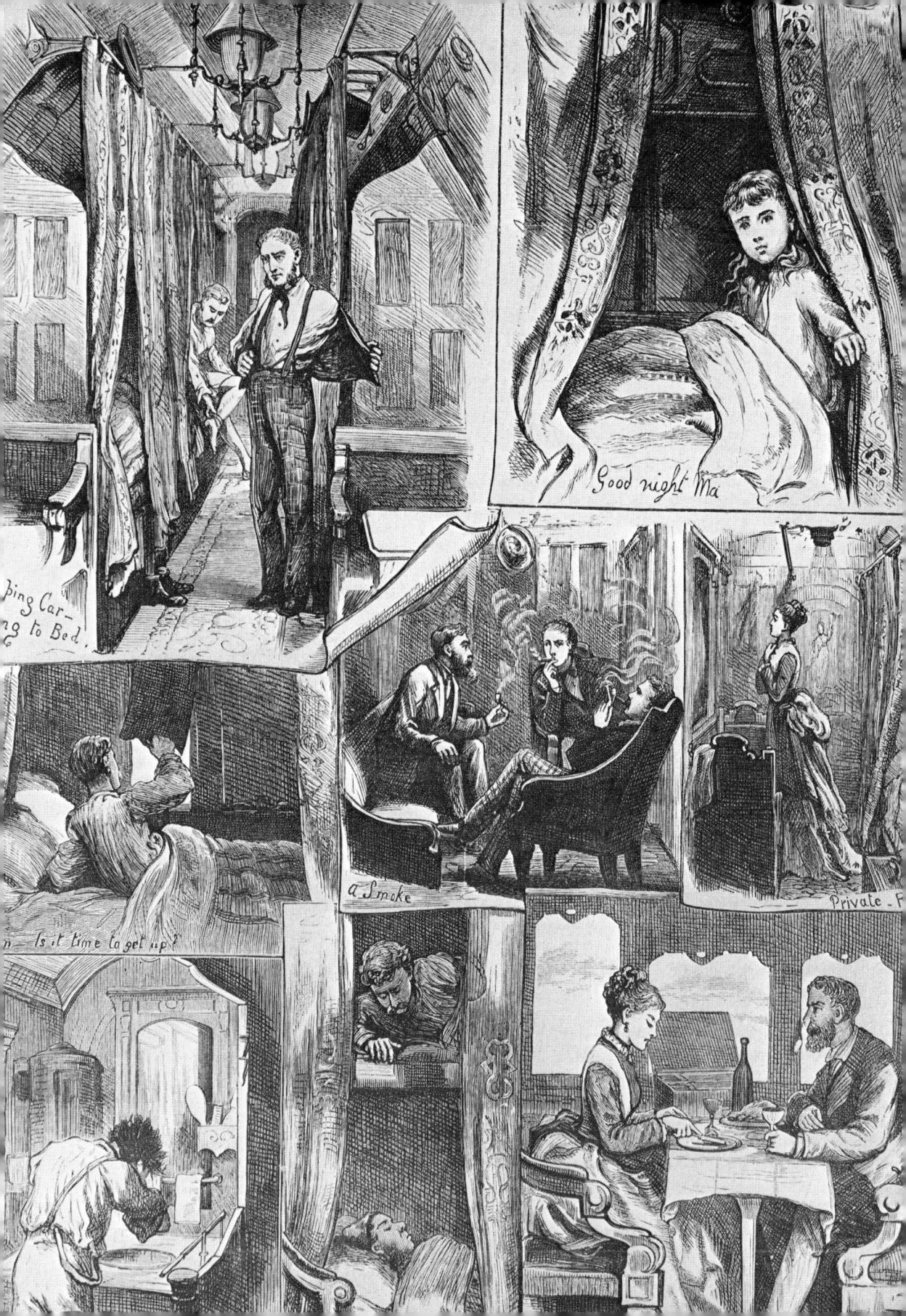

Locomotives

Many 2-2-2 engines were used during this period. They sometimes had a single pair of driving wheels or else they used coupled wheels. They increased in weight and size. In the 1860's steel came to replace iron in construction, being used for boilers, piston rods, axles, etc. When used in the building of wheels it improved the wearing qualities. A tyre made from Bessemer steel could well last for 100,000 miles.

An apparatus was devised which allowed water to be picked up from troughs by locomotives while they were travelling at speed. It cut the whole time needed for taking water to the tender.

A number of tank engines were built for goods and passenger work. They were often used on local lines.

Among the engine designers of the time were men whose names have become famous in railway history. They include Stroudley, Stirling, Webb and Wainwright.

Pullman Cars

Pullman cars came from America and were introduced into Britain by the Midland Railway in 1874. They came in sections, by sea and were put together at Derby. The first Pullmans had a buffet or travelling bar.

By the early years of the present century the London, Brighton & South Coast Railway ran an all Pullman train, the *Southern Belle*, a most luxurious means of travel:

> It is heated with hot water, and installed with electric bells, electric light, and electric ventilation . . . It is a handsome train, well worth the twelve shillings, that is less than three-halfpence a mile, for the double ride in it, and it travels well, giving a really comfortable run of the fifty miles within the hour.[1]

Railway Races

As speeds increased, different companies competed to encourage customers to use their trains. A famous series of races was held in 1895 on the route to Aberdeen. The North Eastern, Great Northern and North British Railways worked the East coast route while the London and North Western and the Caledonian Railway ran on the West coast route.

On 20 August the East coast express covered the 523 miles from London to Aberdeen in 8 hours 40 minutes, an average of over 60 m.p.h. The following night a West coast express travelled a route 17 miles longer in 8 hours 32 minutes, but with a lighter train. The rivalry was intense; it is difficult to say who was the winner.

Royal Trains

As her reign progressed Queen Victoria made regular use of the railway. Extra safety precautions were taken for her and one return journey from London to Balmoral in the 1880's cost about £5000, with a look-out man posted every 200 yards. Her journeys were a good advertisement for railway companies.

By the early years of this century the Royal Train on the Great Northern route was remarkable:

> This is a complete little flat on wheels, designed so as to give a wonderful amount of accommodation . . . The entrance doors are double, and the windows are of bevelled plate-glass balanced so that they can be easily adjusted to any required height. Entrance balcony, smoke-room, day-saloon, dining-room by day or bedroom by night, dressing room, and attendant's compartment, come in due order.[2]

Sleeping Cars

Generally, journeys in Britain were not so long as those in some other lands so there was not an urgent need for sleeping accommodation on trains. However in 1873 several railways began using them. The North Western introduced a 33ft sleeping carriage on to its West coast route to Glasgow. In each compartment four day seats converted into two beds, while two hammocks could be let down from the roof.

Now answer these questions:
1. *What were the first brakes used on trains?*
2. *Name four of Britain's main railway companies in 1914.*
3. *What was a Pullman car?*
4. *From which date were sleeping cars used on Britain's railways?*

[1]Source unknown
[2]Source unknown

10. Railways Abroad, before 1914

Railways were pioneered in Britain. They are generally acknowledged as a British invention. It was not long, however, before other countries became deeply interested in the new form of transport and introduced it. By 1914 thousands of miles of line had been built in all of the world's continents. Some lands established systems far greater in length and complexity than that existing in Britain.

During the Victorian Age British power grew overseas. The Empire was extended to include thousands of square miles of territory. A major motive for this development was the desire to expand trade. Lands in some parts of the world could provide vast resources of raw materials which Britain herself lacked. When these had been manufactured into goods, the inhabitants of such territories could become customers. They would buy the products of Sheffield or Manchester or Glasgow. In the same way that railways helped trade within the British Isles, they assisted industry and commerce throughout the Empire.

Engineers who had gained experience in building lines in Britain went abroad to construct railways in Imperial territories. Often they faced great difficulties. There were vast distances to cover, high mountains to tunnel through and enormous swamps to cross. In Canada, for example, the Rocky Mountains presented a giant barrier. From the 1850's hundreds of miles of line were laid across the wide areas of Australia. India, South Africa and New Zealand all had railways built, sometimes involving very remarkable feats of engineering, with long bridges across wide gorges. Occasionally, sharp gradients were used to carry the lines thousands of feet above sea level.

Fig. 26. A French express on the Paris-Orléans railway, c. 1890.

Fig. 27. A busy railroad on the Erie Railway, New York State, 1874.

In India almost 5000 miles of line had been laid by 1870. This figure had risen to more than 30,000 miles by the outbreak of the First World War. The railways there were a help to commerce within the country. Also, they enabled British officials to govern more easily.

One of the most famous tracks laid in the Empire was the Canadian Pacific Railway. It traversed the country and helped trade to develop. The first trans-continental train ran in 1886.

The railway had existed in North America since the 1830's. The great size of the United States meant that trains became an extremely useful method of transport there. Thousands of miles of track were laid; by the 1880's there were almost 200,000 miles in existence. During one year, 1887, nearly 13,000 miles of line were set down.

The railroad opened up the great middle areas of the United States after 1870. Farming produce was transported quickly by freight trains to the ports of the east coast. From there it was shipped to Europe, bringing great prosperity to America's farmers and traders.

There were considerable differences between the American railway network and that of Great Britain. For example, sections of line were laid under direct opposition from Indian tribes. The Pawnees, Sioux and Blackfeet particularly resented the white man's invasion of their lands and attacked the gangs of labourers who brought the new transport westwards in the 1860's and 1870's.

The vast distances involved in travelling across the United States led to the development of facilities for eating and sleeping whilst on trains. Such provision was needed more there than in a small country like England. By the early 1860's George M. Pullman had designed and produced a sleeping car in which passengers could travel comfortably.

Fig. 28. A military train in French West Africa, 1892.

Care was taken also to provide food and refreshment for passengers engaged on long journeys.

On the Continent of Europe railways were built in the 1830's and 1840's. However, it was not until the 1870's that railway construction began on a large scale. This was later than the development in Britain. Sometimes British engineers were called in to organise the work. One was the famous contractor, Thomas Brassey who laid down stretches of line in France. He took with him gangs of navvies to dig tunnels and cuttings, erect bridges and viaducts.

Sections of railway lines were built in many European countries. In France, Austria, Italy and Belgium, for example people were able to see and use the wonderful, though rather frightening new locomotives. They made travel across the continent far swifter and more comfortable than it had been in the coaching days. By 1914 railways had also a more sinister use. They enabled soldiers to be moved rapidly to war fronts.

Now try to answer these questions:
1. *How did railways help Britain to trade with her Empire?*
2. *How did North America's railways affect British farmers?*
3. *When did large scale railway building begin in Europe?*

11. Railways at War, 1914–1918

Britain's railway system was built in a period of peace and was intended to serve a civilian world. However, such a rapid method of transport was obviously of use to military forces. During the 19th century a number of countries moved their armies by rail during campaigns. Troops could be transferred quickly from one area of fighting to another. A good example was seen during the Franco-Prussian War of 1870 when the German railway system was put into efficient use to carry armies to the front.

From 1871 an order was made in Britain which would bring the railways under the control of the government in time of national emergency. As the international situation grew worse in the years leading down to 1914, plans were made by the various British companies to make timetables which could be used in war. The General Managers of the leading railway companies were consulted and drew up schemes to be put into operation at short notice.

Britain was drawn into the war when German forces invaded Belgium. A British ultimatum was rejected and at midnight on 4 August 1914 the nation entered a conflict which was to last for more than four years.

The plans laid beforehand were put into effect. They had foreseen that the bulk of the extra effort would have to be made by railways in the southern half of Britain. Thousands of men and hundreds of tons of war materials were moved to such ports as Portsmouth, Dover and Southampton. From there

Fig. 29. A British train in France, c. 1916.

they crossed over to France without any accident occurring. Almost 700 special trains were needed to carry 125,000 men and their equipment in this first great operation. It received priority over other traffic:

TRAFFIC BY PASSENGER TRAIN

Notice is hereby given that in consequence of the European war crisis the regular passenger train and boat services usually run by the railway companies may be considerably curtailed or interrupted, and that traffic can only be accepted as it can be dealt with and then only on the understanding that responsibility will not be accepted for any delay, damage or loss which may arise through any such curtailment or interruption.

By Order of

The Executive Committee[1]

On the Western Front, in Northern France, the war stagnated by the end of 1914. Millions of men faced each other from strongly fortified positions in trenches. There was hardly any movement. Casualties were stupendous. Forces needed thousands of tons of supplies and these were often taken to areas near the front line by train.

Special units of the British Army were formed to build, maintain and operate railways in the sector containing the British Expeditionary Force. Locomotives and rolling stock were shipped over the English Channel and used to carry men, weapons and ammunition to the front line, and wounded soldiers out to base hospitals.

British stock was seen in many parts of the World during the War. Some North Western engines finished their lives in the Middle East. A number of Great Western 0-6-0's were sent to Salonika. Some L.S.W.R. locomotives reached Mesopotamia.

At home, services were well maintained until the end of 1916. Then as the gruelling war dragged on, grim cuts became necessary for civilians. Coal was needed for the war effort, there were staff shortages and some locomotives were required overseas.

When the war broke out, the railways of Britain had staffs which numbered about 600,000 men.

[1]Announcement by the Railway Executive Committee, 8th August 1914, quoted in *Britain's Railways in World War I*, by J. A. B. Hamilton

Fig. 30. A munitions train in the First World War.

Thousands of these joined the army and navy and served on many fronts. More than 21,000 died. Their jobs at home were filled, where possible, by older men or by women.

Some women had been employed by railways before 1914, often as servants in companies' hotels. As men left to join up, more women took over. By the end of the war, almost 70,000 women were at work, helping to keep rail transport flowing smoothly. What jobs did they do? Some were clerks, others were porters, others again were carriage cleaners or guards. Their efforts helped Britain's railways to run good services during the war years. In 1918, after the end of the fighting, the women left their jobs which were taken over by the returning servicemen.

For the first time in warfare, attacks were made from the air. Aircraft had been developed to carry bombs and from 1915 German planes launched raids on various parts of Britain. Special precautions had to be taken by railway companies:

Passengers in railway carriages which are provided with blinds MUST keep the blinds lowered so as to cover the windows. The blinds may be lifted in case of necessity when the train is at a standstill at a station, but if lifted must be lowered again before the train starts.[1]

All through the war there was a heavy railway traffic between London and ports on the south coast. Leave trains carried troops coming on leave from the battlefront. Victoria Station became famous as a centre from which soldiers returned to France. Ambulance trains carried the wounded home to hospitals in Britain. On some occasions men who were wounded in attacks at dawn reached London by the early afternoon.

By 1918 Britain's railways had served well and contributed towards the successful conclusion of the war.

During the war there occurred the worst accident of Britain's railway history. It happened in 1915 when a troop train crashed at Quintinshill, on the Caledonian Railway. (see p. 64)

Can you now answer the questions that follow?
1. *What was the first important task that Britain's railways had to carry out after war had been declared in 1914?*
2. *Name one railway whose engines were sent abroad.*
3. *How many railwaymen were killed in action during the war?*
4. *Name two jobs carried out by women on Britain's railways between 1914 and 1918.*
5. *What was a leave train?*

[1]Command Order, Dec. 1915, quoted in the same.

Fig. 31. The 'Schools' Class Engine, St Olave's.

12. Railways, 1918–1939

The pressures of war upon Britain's railway system were very great. It had not been possible to maintain all track and equipment in first class order. Because factories had been turning out munitions for the war effort, there had not been adequate replacement of rolling stock. Some of the engines, carriages and trucks which were in use in 1918 should have been scrapped long before that time.

It was decided to reform Britain's railways by amalgamating them in several groups. After the war there were still 120 companies. In Parliament a Railways Amalgamation Act was passed in 1921. It arranged that four large companies should come into operation from January 1923. They were the London and North Eastern Railway, the London, Midland and Scottish Railway, the Great Western Railway and the Southern Railway.

The largest of the companies was the L.M.S.R. It took in 7 constituent and 27 subsidiary companies. These included the London and North Western, the famous Midland Railway, the Highland Railway in Scotland and the Cockermouth, Keswick and Penrith line in Cumberland. Its route mileage became more than 6700. Routes ran from London to the far north of Scotland, running up the western side of England. Distances were great for British railways, as a journey from Euston to Wick covered 730 miles. The colour adopted for stock was the old Midland red.

Second largest of the new companies was the L.N.E.R., whose system covered eastern England and eastern and western Scotland. It took in some of the areas where the first railways had been built. Among the lines included were the old Great Central and Great Eastern railways. The colour chosen for locomotives was light green, with a light shade of brown for coaches.

The Great Western Railway was the third of the new companies. Its own history went back to the early days of railway construction in the 19th century. By the terms of amalgamation some lines in Wales, including the Cambrian Railway were included. The G.W.R. covered the west of England with its services, running dark green locomotives and brown and cream coaches.

The smallest of the new companies was the Southern Railway whose green coloured stock ran on a route of just over 2000 miles. However, in spite of its comparatively short distances, the running traffic on the S.R. was very concentrated, taking in the London suburban services. Among the older companies which made up the Southern were the London, Brighton and South Coast and the South Eastern and Chatham Railway.

The four new lines were faced with large problems. Before 1914, railways had had a monopoly of long distance transport. People travelling from Scotland to the Midlands or Lancashire to London had used train services. But after 1918 there came increasing competition from motor transport.

Motor vehicles powered by internal combustion engines increased rapidly in number. In 1922 for example, there were 315,000 private cars and 151,000 commercial vehicles. Eight years later these figures had risen to 1 million and 334,000 respectively.

Many people came to own cars. Others travelled by bus or long distance coach services. Often these proved to be more convenient than travel by train. They could offer a door-to-door service.

Railway goods traffic declined. Farm products were taken from the country to towns and cities by lorry. It was more direct. Cargoes from ships were sometimes transported directly from docks to markets by road. Railway companies suffered financially and their shareholders received small dividends as return for their investments.

To meet the competition, railways were themselves allowed, after 1928, to own fleets of lorries. Thus they were able to link road and rail services to carry goods about the country.

A new method of power was introduced in some urban areas. It was pioneered particularly by the Southern Railway. During the 1930's electrified lines were extended from London to such places as Brighton, Portsmouth and Hastings. Electric trains were used to advantage on journeys which involved stops at a number of stations. They could gather speed more easily and rapidly, thus local services were speeded up.

During this period the development of the steam engine as a means of power was improved. The strength of boilers was increased so that steam pressures could be raised. Some experiments were

Fig. 32. The Cheltenham Flyer in the 1920's.

made in streamlining. Thus, speeds and performances were improved.

On the Great Western Railway two classes of engine reached particular fame. They were the 'Castles' and the 'Kings'. Their performances brought the G.W.R. a reputation for fast running speeds. For example, in 1932 the *Cheltenham Flyer* covered the 77 miles from Swindon to Paddington at an average speed of more than 81 m.p.h., in 56 mins. 47 secs.

The London, and North Eastern Railway introduced streamlined designs into some of its locomotives. The designer was Sir Nigel Gresley. In 1935 the *Silver Jubilee* express pulled by the engine *Silver Link*, created several world speed records on the run from London to Newcastle. On 27 September 1935 the 103-ton locomotive twice reached a maximum speed of $112\frac{1}{2}$ m.p.h. In 1938 one of Gresley's steam locomotives, the streamlined *Mallard*, attained a world steam speed record when it touched 126 m.p.h. for a short time.

Improvements were made to systems of signalling, track laying and general maintenance by all four railways. Power was introduced in some places to control signal systems. Elsewhere, colour signals were used.

Passengers' comfort was added to by the building of better carriages. More corridor coaches were provided, often with lavatories. Restaurant cars were attached to more trains so that travellers could obtain meals when making journeys. Steel was used in constructing underframes and for side plating to give greater strength to

Fig. 33. A busy station scene between the wars, Paddington 1932.

carriages. Electric lighting, generated by a dynamo under the coach, was provided to all compartments.

But in spite of these improvements and developments on Britain's railways during this period, they suffered in comparison with the enormous expansion of transport by road. In 1939 they once again had to face up to the demands of war.

By answering the following questions you will learn more about this subject:

1. *Why were Britain's railways amalgamated into four large companies after 1918?*
2. *Why did railways meet with greater competition from other forms of transport between the wars?*

13. Some Aspects of Railways, 1918–1939

This chapter deals with some aspects of railways during the period between 1918 and 1939.

Comfort

When there was increased competition from other forms of transport, it became necessary for railways to offer greater comfort to their passengers. Inside carriages more room was made for them by reducing the number of compartments and improving the seating. On some lines, arm rests were provided for third class passengers. But this meant that trains had to be larger in order to take the number of people whom they had previously carried in less comfort.

Restaurant accommodation became important on trains. In the 1930's the *Royal Scot* of the L.M.S. carried two kitchen carriages, two third class restaurant cars and two half sections of first class restaurant cars.

For those passengers who were travelling overnight, sleeping carriages were provided. First class compartments contained single bedrooms and about nine or ten passengers were taken in each carriage. In the third class, the 'sleeper' weighed about 35 tons and generally carried 28 passengers in four-berth compartments.

Bogie wheel suspension was made better to give greater comfort. Steel springs and rubber gave a smooth ride for travellers. The old four and six wheeled coaches had disappeared and the bogies were each mounted on four or six wheels.

Electrification

Electric power had a number of advantages over steam power as a means of driving trains. During the period between the wars a considerable mileage of line in Britain was electrified. This happened particularly in the suburban areas near to London.

Mainly involved was the Southern Railway which had brought electric power to several hundred miles of route by 1939. It then had the largest urban electrified scheme in the World.

Two of the companies which went to form the Southern Railway in 1923 had already introduced electric trains. They were the London, Brighton and South Coast Railway and the London and South Western Railway. However, each had used a different method.

The L.B. & S.C.R. had employed an overhead system, giving 6000 volts A.C. The L. & S.W.R. had used a third rail at ground level, giving 650 volts D.C. The Southern Railway chose the second system and equipped all of its electrified line with 'live' rail.

Power came from electricity sub-stations at the side of the line. The train was driven by a driver who sat holding a handle, known as the 'Dead Man's Handle'. It was a safety measure. All the time the driver kept the handle pressed down, the train operated. If the handle was released, as it would be if the driver became ill, the brakes were applied automatically.

Famous Trains

During this period, some very famous trains ran on the lines of the four companies.

One of the best known was the *Royal Scot* of the L.M.S.R. It left Euston at 10 a.m. each day bound for Scotland, pulling some 450 tons of weight behind the engine. The train was made up of three sections, going to Glasgow, Edinburgh and Aberdeen respectively. The journey to Glasgow took less than 8 hours.

Equally famous was the *Flying Scotsman* of the L.N.E.R., which began as a service in 1862. At 10 a.m. each morning, trains left Kings Cross, London and Waverley Station, Edinburgh, each bound for the other terminus. In the 1930's the journeys were made in about 7¾ hours. One of the special services provided on the train was a hairdressing saloon!

For a period of years the G.W.R. ran the World's fastest train. It was the *Cheltenham Flyer*, which could manage the start to finish journey at over 75½ m.p.h. The engines used were of the 'Castle' class.

The railway nearest to the Continent was the Southern and it had one of the most luxurious trains ever seen. This was the *Golden Arrow* which ran between London and Paris. At Dover, passengers crossed the Channel by ship, then boarded the

Fig. 34. First Class coaches in the 1920's.

Fig. 35. S.R. electric train in the 1930's on the Waterloo-Portsmouth line.

Fig. 36. The Mallard.

Fig. 37. (right) Platelayers at work, on the G.W.R., 1930.

French half of the train at Calais, to journey to Paris. The *Golden Arrow* was made up of Pullman cars and for some time consisted only of first class accommodation.

The same railway also introduced an electric express, the *Brighton Belle*, which covered the 51 miles from Victoria Station to the coast in about an hour. The five carriages, each weighing 62 tons, were fitted luxuriously.

Locomotive classes

The years from 1919 to 1939 were the heyday of steam as a driving power for trains. Some classes of engine were built which were famous in railway history. The L.N.E.R. used some giant 'Pacific' locomotives, which were 4-6-2 in wheel arrangement. The 'Shire' class were 4-4-0.

On the L.M.S.R. the 'Royal Scots' were 4-6-0. By the middle of the period, the railway had about 230 4-4-0 compound locomotives which gave excellent service.

The G.W.R. had the 'Castles' and 'Kings' to maintain its reputation for speed. They were both 4-6-0 in design.

The Southern used 'King Arthurs' and 'Lord Nelsons', both 4-6-0. Also they introduced the remarkable 'Schools' class of 4-4-0 design and great power.

Among the engineers who built these different types of locomotives were H. N. Gresley, W. A. Stainer, C. B. Collett and R. E. L. Maunsell.

All railways used tank engines for shorter journeys. They had certain advantages in the working of trains on smaller local lines.

Permanent Way

The speeds achieved by trains weighing hundreds of tons put great pressure on rails. Their construction and upkeep has been, all through railway history, an aspect of work that is often overlooked. There were two main types of rail used. The one usually laid down by British companies was the 'bull-head' rail, so called because of its shape. It was fixed into a metal 'chair', which in turn was fixed to wooden sleepers. Many other lands used the flat-bottomed rail which fitted into steel sole plates on the sleepers.

British rails were laid usually in 60 ft lengths, with a weight of 95 lb. per yard. The rails were joined by 'fishplates'. The setting and upkeep of the permanent way was a hard and exacting task which had to be carried out in all weathers by platelayers.

To give some idea of their responsibility, one mile of track contained 176 rails, more than 4000 'chairs' and over 2000 wooden 'sleepers'. All railways kept a steady watch on the safety of their track.

Without looking back at the chapter which you have just read, can you now answer these questions?

1. *Give one example of greater comfort provided for passengers in this period.*
2. *Which railway company carried out most electrification?*
3. *What were the two methods of electrification?*
4. *How did the 'Dead Man's Handle' work?*
5. *Which railway ran the* Cheltenham Flyer*?*
6. *Name one of the famous locomotive engineers of the period.*

14. Railways at War, 1939–1945

When the Second World War broke out in 1939, Britain's railways were once again put at the disposal of the government. A first task was to transport the British Expeditionary Force to France. Many divisions of soldiers had to be taken by train from their camps to the Channel ports. Their equipment had also to be carried. Lorries, tanks, guns and ammunition were moved on their way to the Western Front.

Many civilian services were curtailed. Expresses were taken off and priority was given to troop trains. At night special precautions had to be taken so that lights did not show. Dark blue bulbs were fitted in passenger compartments and blinds were kept down.

Great demands were made on railways in the south of England during the summer of 1940. On the Continent the German armies broke through and British forces were pinned back on the port of Dunkirk in northern France. About 336,000 men were evacuated by sea, and landed in England. A massive railway operation was mounted to transport the tired men to centres all over Britain. More than 600 special trains were used.

By August German air attacks were increasing as the Battle of Britain raged in the skies. The development of aircraft within a few years meant that they could play an important part in war. The railways of southern England were within easy reach of the Luftwaffe's airfields in France and the Low Countries. Therefore attacks were frequent. To counter them, train drivers were ordered to proceed at a reduced speed when air raid signals were given. This led to an amount of chaos. Travellers found that their journeys, though fairly short in distance, sometimes lasted for several hours.

Towards the end of the year, speed restrictions were relaxed. But then began the heavy night bombing known as 'the Blitz'. A number of British cities, especially London, were attacked during the hours of darkness and heavy damage resulted. Incendiary bombs caused many fires on railway premises. High explosives damaged engines, carriages and sometimes destroyed lengths of track. Early in 1941, Southwark Street Bridge was hit by a parachute mine and its eight lines were blocked. The railway staff worked bravely, often in conditions of considerable danger, to keep trains running and to repair damage. Some attacks were directed at goods yards where hundreds of trucks made a fine target for bomb-aimers.

Britain's railway system found itself faced by other problems. Greater demands were made upon it as a means of travel both for passengers and freight. There was a shortage of petrol, therefore few people used road transport. The English Channel and the ports of the east coast could not be used by coastal steamers as they had before 1939. Therefore coal and other commodities had to be carried by rail to those areas. Industry, the Army, the Navy and the Air Force all had urgent and special demands for moving men and materials. The railway service was hard pressed to meet their requirements. In 1941 alone, more than 10,000 trains left Britain's Midland and North-Eastern coalfields, carrying their cargoes to various parts of the country.

As railwaymen were called to the armed forces, many women came to take their places in certain jobs. For example, at some stations they were employed as clerks, selling tickets, or as carriage cleaners, or as porters.

By the early part of 1944 Britain was a vast armed camp. Hundreds of thousands of servicemen were gathered ready for the invasion of Europe. They were concentrated mainly in an area of southern England, preparing for D-Day. When it began, on 6 June, there was heavy rail traffic to Southampton, carrying a stream of men and supplies. Just afterwards, about 100,000 troops were moved by rail in less than a week. Civilian traffic was heavily cut to make way for the special trains.

Under such pressure Britain's railways suffered. It was difficult to obtain new stock and spare parts. Although more than £1 million was spent on improvements to railways, it did not keep pace with the wear and tear suffered. Yet in spite of these difficulties some progress was made in design and development of locomotives. For example, H. A. V. Bulleid of the Southern Railway produced and developed the 'Merchant Navy' class of passenger express engine, which was in use until the last days of steam.

Britain's railway companies had made a large

Fig. 38. Bomb damage at Clapham Junction. September 1940.

Fig. 39. Tanks being transported by train.

contribution to the successful running of the war. Air attacks had killed some 900 people, of whom 400 were railwaymen. More than 100 employees won decorations for showing heroism when under attack.

Here are four questions for you to attempt:

1. *Why were railways in southern England very important at the beginning of the war?*
2. *Give three examples of the difficulties experienced by Britain's railways during the war.*
3. *Did aerial bombing attacks affect railways near to where you live?*
4. *Who designed the 'Merchant Navy' class of locomotives?*

15. Railways since 1945

At the end of the Second World War, Britain's railway system was in need of much new investment. During the preceding six years there had been few replacements of stock. Necessary repairs had been delayed and railways could not offer the comfort and efficiency that were needed to run a system of transport well.

In 1945 a Labour Government was elected to power. It announced that it would take the railways under State control and ownership—that is, to nationalise them. Therefore, the government bought out the four companies and intended to invest capital in them. The nationalisation took place in 1948.

The four large companies—L.N.E.R., L.M.S.R., G.W.R., and S.R. were taken over by a Railway Executive which was to run them. The Executive was part of the British Transport Commission which controlled many forms of the country's mechanised transport. But there had to be some division of the new, giant British Railways. It was too large to run as one company. Therefore there was a division into six areas. These were known as regions and were the Southern, the Western, the Eastern, the London Midland, the North Eastern and the Scottish. Gradually each region has organised more and more of its own programme of services.

But ever since 1948 the railways have failed to develop as a profitable method of transport. In fact

Fig. 40. Dr R. Beeching with his Report, 1963.

they have run at a loss and have gone deeper and deeper into debt. To meet these losses, the State has had to pay money each year. It is known as a subsidy. Why have Britain's railways failed to flourish?

Mainly, they have had to face great competition from other forms of transport. In particular there has been a vast increase in the numbers of motor vehicles used. The British motor industry expanded its production. In 1945, about $1\frac{1}{2}$ million cars were registered in Great Britain. Within eleven years this number had risen to nearly four million. Ten years later the figure was approaching eight million.

The country's increasing wealth has been shown partly by the buying of cars and vans. Many people have found them to be a more direct method of personal transport than trains. When used for business or for pleasure they have certain definite advantages over rail travel. Can you name them? But can you also list their disadvantages today?

Lorries and coaches have continued to take freight and passenger traffic from railways. By-passes and motorways have been built and have enabled these forms of transport to move their cargoes about at speed. One of the advantages of railways, that is rapidity, has been partly offset by motorway construction.

Another competitor in the field of transport has been air travel. Since the end of the Second World War thousands of aircraft have been built. It is well known that they have been widely used for travel between different countries. What is perhaps not so widely recognised is that the aeroplane is often employed for travel within the British Isles. Thousands of people have found it a rapid means of getting from place to place. For example a businessman from London may wish to visit a branch of his company in Edinburgh. He could travel on a train, taking six or seven hours. Or he could fly there in less than two hours. It is obvious which method the busy executive is more likely to choose.

By the mid-1950's Britain's railways were losing so much money that steps had to be taken to modernise them. By 1962 the loss was about £160,000,000 annually; that works out at some £18,000 per hour! Railways had been built in the first place as part of the revolution brought about

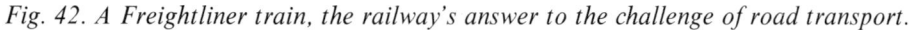

Fig. 41. Station car park. Competitors or partners? Commuters' cars in Harlow Town.

Fig. 42. A Freightliner train, the railway's answer to the challenge of road transport.

Fig. 43. A closed branch line in Kent.

by the invention of the steam engine. Steam power was easily available. There were enormous supplies of coal and iron.

However it was decided to alter the method of power used in locomotives. A plan was announced for changing over to diesel engines and electricity. After some 120 years of steam it was hard for many people to accept that its days were numbered. Gradually the new forms of power were introduced. They were more efficient than steam.

It was obvious that Britain's railways needed a drastic overhaul and re-organisation. Therefore the government appointed Dr Richard Beeching to investigate them. His Report was published in 1963 and made various suggestions for improving the system. He pointed out that railway building during the 19th century had been haphazard. Too many lines had been built. Dr Beeching recommended that many small branch lines should be closed down. They were not paying their way because of the increased use of motor cars in rural areas. He also suggested that main line services should be improved. The reaction to the Report was mixed. Some people welcomed it as the only way to save Britain's railways from extinction. Others claimed that by 'axing' so many services country areas were being deprived of vital transport and many railwaymen were facing unemployment.

Parts of the Beeching Plan have been put into effect. A number of closures have taken place.

Measures are being taken to make Britain's railways more efficient.

But the basic difficulties remain. Most countries have expanded their use of railways since 1945, carrying more passengers and goods traffic. But in Britain the pattern has been different. Fewer people and firms have made use of rail transport:

> Receipts from passenger and freight train traffic in 1965 amounted to £457 million, a fall of about £2 million compared with the previous year. Passenger receipts were higher, but these gains were more than offset by a decline in freight revenue, largely caused by a significant drop in the tonnage of coal carried . . .[1]

Staff have been reduced in numbers, as the following figures show:

Year	Staff
1948	648,740
1953	594,292
1958	550,123
1963	439,551
1965	365,043

Now find the answers to the following questions:
1. *What does the word 'nationalisation' mean?*
2. *How many regions were formed by British Railways?*
3. *Give examples of the competition which has faced Britain's railway system since 1948.*

[1] From *Facts and Figures of British Rail*, 1965

16. Some Aspects of Railways, since 1945

This chapter deals with various aspects of Britain's railways since the end of the Second World War.

Carriages

Since 1945 the number of carriages in use remained fairly steady until the early 1960's. Then it began to decline. However, a large amount of new stock has been built. There are now two classes of travel, first class and second class; the latter is the old third class renamed. Carriages have steel underframes and body frames and are comfortable. For example, the standard second class carriage has eight compartments and the seats are fitted with arm rests. Therefore only 48 passengers are accommodated and travel is made more pleasant.

Coaches on trains provide increasingly for the rising standards of living of the British people. Restaurant and buffet cars are available for those wishing to eat or drink on the journey. Sleeping coaches have been improved to provide an excellent service for passengers who have to travel overnight.

Travel is far less comfortable in the urban areas. The busy times occur during the morning and early evening periods, when hundreds of thousands of people flock to and from their work. Stations and trains are used to capacity but most passengers accept the fact that the service cannot be extended. Travel can be very uncomfortable at those peak times.

The Channel Tunnel

One of the greatest differences between life today and that of previous ages is the amount people travel. For example, each year thousands of them leave Britain to spend holidays abroad; thousands of foreigners come to these shores. Travellers cross the English Channel by sea or by air.

The Channel was for generations a vital part of Britain's defences, holding possible conquerors at bay, as if behind a moat. But now the 21 miles of sea is a hindrance to trade and passenger travel between Britain and the mainland of Europe. Therefore schemes have been proposed in recent years to build a direct link with the Continent.

The most popular idea has been for a Channel Tunnel. One was begun at the end of the last century but the workings have lain derelict for many years. The new tunnel will run through layers of rock under the sea. It will have railway tracks so that passengers and freight will be carried by train; the idea of a road tunnel or bridge has been ruled out. Cars will be transported on trucks.

The twin tunnels will be just over 21 feet in diameter and about 32 miles in length, linking the British and French railway systems. Express trains will be able to hurtle through the tunnel at speeds of up to 90 m.p.h., carrying passengers at great speed directly from London to Paris, Brussels and other large European cities.

The Channel Tunnel will offer an enormous opportunity to British Rail to extend its passenger and freight services.

Diesel Trains

Dr Rudolf Diesel, a German, worked on the production of the first engines which bear his name, during the 1890's. They are a form of internal combustion engine. In the cylinder a fine spray of oil is ignited by the high temperature of compressed air. Thus an explosive stroke moves the piston and works the engine.

From that time, experiments were made to use diesel engines in various forms of transport. During the 1930's the first attempts were made with diesel rail traction in Britain. But it was not until the period after 1945 that wider use was made of diesel power. When British Rail's modernisation scheme was introduced in 1955, it allowed for a widespread introduction of diesel locomotives. Overall they have a number of advantages over steam engines. They are easier to work and are cleaner. Which other advantages can you think of? In 1965, 2,811 were in service.

Electrification

Electric trains were in wide use before 1945. Since that year there has been an expansion of their use. Unlike steam and diesel engines they do not have to carry their own fuel with them. However, this can

Fig. 44. A comfortable modern carriage.

also be a disadvantage, because they can run only when electric current is provided. But overall, they have great potential as a method of transport.

The power comes to the engine either from a third rail or from overhead wires. Both types are found on Britain's railways and have been extended since the end of the war. By 1966 a fast electric service was operating between London, Manchester and Liverpool.

Monorail

Different types of transport rely on each other. An interesting possibility for the future of Britain's railways is the building of overhead monorails. Railcars can travel on these at high speed. They would be very valuable in transporting passengers to and from airports. At present the journey is often made by road, involving slow travel on many occasions.

By monorail it would be possible to carry people at a speed of 150 m.p.h., in great safety, to their waiting aircraft and to bring returning passengers straight to the heart of a city.

Nationalisation

A General Election was held in 1945 and was won by the Labour Party. The new government announced that it would nationalise all heavy transport. The Transport Act for carrying out this policy was passed and Part II of the Act, taking the railways under State control, took effect on 1st January 1948. The four companies which had worked since 1923 then became British Railways, later named British Rail, with over almost 20,000 miles of route and a staff of about 700,000.

Fig. 45. *An electric express on the London-Manchester line speeds alongside the M.1 motorway.*

Staff

Since 1945 there has been a steady decline in the number of staff employed by British Railways. In 1949 there were just over 624,000 men and women. Ten years later this number had dropped by more than one hundred thousand and in 1965 the total stood at 365,000.

As railways have closed branch lines and have cut some services, fewer people have been needed to run them. The change from steam for locomotives to diesel and electric power has led to a reduction in footplate staff, for firemen are no longer needed.

Here is an analysis of British Rail's staff at the end of 1965:

Salaried staff	84,935
Wage earning staff:	
Operations	
Drivers, firemen and cleaners	47,352
Guards, signalmen, shunters, porters, ticket collectors, etc.	73,405
Goods and cartage	29,221
Running shed, carriage and wagon cleaning, etc.	16,091
Maintenance and construction	
Conciliation	35,838
Workshop	71,731
Miscellaneous	6,470
	365,043[1]

Steam Locomotives

In 1948 there were more than 20,000 steam locomotives in use on Britain's railway system. Twenty

[1] From Facts and Figures of British Rail, 1965.

Fig. 46. One of the last steam trains leaving Paddington Station.

years later the last one made the final journey by steam power on British Rail. The new Industrial Revolution is based upon more modern methods of traction for railway engines. Diesel and electric power have been used.

Since the end of the Second World War, Britain's coal production has decreased. In many areas, steam power is no longer required for industry.

For a few years after 1945 improvements were made in the design and performances of steam locomotives. Experiments were carried out in streamlining. Some fast runs were made by the 'A.4' Pacifics in the North Eastern Region and Bulleid Pacifics on the Southern Region.

But the days of steam were numbered. Gradually the fine locomotives of the past were scrapped and Britain's railways were re-equipped with the new stock.

Now try to answer the questions below without looking back at the chapter:

1. *Describe the proposed Channel Tunnel*
2. *Name one advantage of electric locomotives over other types.*
3. *When did Britain's railways become the property of the State?*
4. *Why have the numbers of staff employed dropped since 1945?*
5. *How many steam locomotives were in use in 1948?*

17. Railways Abroad, since 1914

Since the beginning of the First World War, the use of railways has expanded over the whole world. They were particularly an invention of the 19th century and in many respects, that period marked their heyday. In the present age they have met increasing competition. First, there has been a gigantic production of motor vehicles, which are now to be seen in every continent. Second, especially since 1945, travellers over long distances have been offered the speedy alternative of air travel, turning a journey of days into one lasting for a few hours only. Yet in spite of these newer forms of transport, railways have been developed in many lands and have come to play a vital part in their economic life.

All over the continent of Europe many miles of line have been built since 1914. France had more than 40,000 miles of track just before the outbreak of the Second World War and Germany nearly as much. Some astonishing work has been achieved in tunnelling. The Simplon No. 2 Tunnel, opened in 1922 is more than 12 miles long. The Appenine Tunnel of the Italian State Railway, opened in 1934 is only one mile shorter.

Experiments have been made to speed up travel. In France there was much destruction during the First World War, but soon fast services were established. Before 1935 the 365 miles from Paris to Bordeaux could be covered in 349 minutes by steam train. The Germans experimented with diesel powered railcars. The *Flying Hamburger* from 1933 established a regular service between Hamburg and Berlin, covering the 178 miles in 138 minutes. Can you work out the average speed on the journey? Often the train had to exceed 100 m.p.h. to maintain its schedule.

The greatest rail speed has been achieved since the end of the Second World War in France. There, electric locomotives have been built, taking their power from overhead lines. During the period 1954–1955 trials were made on various stretches of track. By the end of the first week of tests a speed of 151 m.p.h. had been reached by a 106 ton Co-Co locomotive pulling three coaches which weighed over 100 tons. In March 1955, two locomotives, CC 7107 and BB 9004 each reached a speed of 331

Km. (205.5 miles) per hour. Since that time the French National Railways have offered the world's fastest services.

In Japan, the Japan National Railways (JNR) have run very successfully and profitably in recent years. From 1964 they have operated a super-express service between the cities of Osaka and Tokyo, a distance of 320 miles. The trains regularly run at speeds of over 130 m.p.h.

Another part of the world where rail travel has been developed since 1914 is North America. There are vast distances to be covered. Britain's longest route, from the north of Scotland to the south-western tip of Cornwall is tiny when compared to some of the great trans-continental routes of the United States. Many trains have been built like hotels on wheels, because journeys sometimes last for two or three days. Dining-cars, sleeping compartments and observation saloons are widely used.

The long journeys, sometimes made through mountainous country, demand very powerful locomotives. Stream traction was used for many years, but the experiments with diesel power in the 1930's proved very successful. The United States had vast resources of oil. Compared with British stock, American engines are vast. In 1935 the Chesapeake and Ohio Railroad used a 2-10-4 locomotive which weighed 252 tons without its tender! This giant pulled a load of 141 freight cars weighing more than 9,700 tons on a journey of 236 miles at an average speed of over 22 m.p.h. The Southern Pacific Railroad ran one of its trains regularly over a distance of more than 1000 miles without changing the giant locomotive.

Yet the largest were probably the engines used by the Northern Pacific Railroad for work through the Rocky Mountains. The wheel arrangement of these monsters was 2-8-0 + 0-8-4. Engine and tender weighed just over 500 tons and consumed 18 tons of coal in an hour when working hard.

In more recent years, however, United States railway companies have met greater competition from road and air services. Today, diesel-electric or diesel trains are run on the more important lines.

In other continents the railway has become vital

Fig. 47. (above) A French electric express.

Fig. 48. (below) A giant American steam engine.

Fig. 49. A train on a hill line in India.

to trade and travel. Russia spans two continents. Before the German invasion in 1941 she relied greatly on rail services. During the war, vast areas were devastated by bombing and shellfire. After 1945 enormous efforts were made to rebuild the track systems and restore the country's economic life. Today it is possible to travel from Russia's western frontiers in Europe right across to Vladivostok in the east, lying in Asia.

Jungle, desert, plain, mountain, forest—all have been crossed and conquered by railwaymen in many parts of the world. Sometimes the feats of building or railway operation have been stupendous. An example is the Rimutaka Incline, in New Zealand, where as many as five locomotives were needed to drag and haul a train up the 1 in 13 gradient. In Peru, at Volcan Mine, the Peruvian Central Railway reaches an altitude of 15,848 feet.

Today there are well over three quarters of a million miles of track laid in different countries. The gauge varies considerably on main lines from 5ft 6ins in some lands down to 3ft 3⅜ins in others.

Try to answer these questions on overseas railways:

1. *Name two famous tunnels built in Europe since 1914.*
2. *Describe French achievements in electric speed travel.*
3. *Find a picture of a giant American steam locomotive, then compare it with one of a large British engine. What differences can you see?*
4. *Find the names of countries in the world where steam locomotives are still used.*

Fig. 50. A Japanese monorail between Tokyo International Airport and central Tokyo.

18. Underground Railways

The railway revolution of the Victorian Age used up a large amount of land. In towns and cities the new lines often wound their way to a central position, running over viaducts, across bridges, behind houses and under roads. To use up valuable surface areas was a costly business.

Experiments were made with tunnelling in the earth. Several pioneers saw that underground tunnels could be used in transport. In London, underground tubes were designed to run under the River Thames. Marc I. Brunel built the famous Thames Tunnel between 1825 and 1843. He used a boring shield which was rectangular in shape. The tunnel made was then lined with bricks.

Some engineers believed that sub-surface digging could be used to take railway tracks. In some places they would run through deep cuttings. Elsewhere they would tunnel through the earth. Thus the centre of a city could be reached by railway transport.

In the late 1840's one man who formed ideas of building a railway of this kind was Charles Pearson. He was City solicitor and Member of Parliament for Lambeth. When his plan was put forward it was greeted with some ridicule. The humorous magazine *Punch* wrote in 1846:

> We understand that a survey has already been made and that many of the inhabitants along the line have expressed their readiness to place their coal cellars at the disposal of the company. It is believed that much expense may be saved by taking advantage of areas, kitchens, and coal holes already made, through which the trains may run . . .[1]

By 1860 Parliament had agreed to Pearson's scheme for constructing a line underground and the work began. The chief engineer was John Fowler. The undertaking was especially difficult because it ran through an area where houses, roads, gas mains and sewers were already in position. Hundreds of navvies laboured day and night to excavate tunnels, cart away earth and set timbers to hold up the workings.

Pearson died in September 1862, but the Metropolitan Railway which he had founded opened in the following January. A special run was made from Paddington, the Great Western terminus, to Farringdon Street. Among the guests who then sat down to a large banquet was Mr Gladstone. A few days later the *Daily Telegraph* wrote:

> Of the general comfort in travelling on the line there can be no question, and the novel introduction of gas into the carriages is calculated to dispel any unpleasant feeling which passengers, especially ladies, might entertain against riding for so long a distance through a tunnel . . . The second class carriages are nicely fitted with leathered seats, and are very commodious, and the compartments and arms in the first class render overcrowding impossible.[2]

The stock used was from the Great Western Railway as the Metropolitan Railway's own carriages were not ready. Three rails had been laid so that coaches of either broad or standard gauge could be taken. Steam driven locomotives pulled the trains and at times the sulphurous fumes in the tunnels made both passengers and crew feel unwell.

The new line was popular. Many people travelled on it first merely for the novelty. However, they soon found that it offered a rapid and convenient method of transport within the City. During the first week of operation almost 250,000 passengers were carried. The railway flourished. In the first six months of 1865 almost seven and a half million passengers used the Metropolitan.

By the end of 1868 another line had been built and had started services. This was the Metropolitan District Railway which ran at first from Westminster to South Kensington. Other lines were constructed by 1900. Some ran out of London into the surrounding countryside on the surface. Metropolitan trains reached Brill in Buckinghamshire, more than 50 miles from Baker Street.

Steam traction was used in the early days. By the end of the century experiments were being made with the use of electricity as a method of power. It was much cleaner than steam. Both the Metropolitan Railway and the Metropolitan District Railway used electric rails in some areas and electric

[1] *Punch*, 1846

[2] *Daily Telegraph*, 12th Jan. 1863

Fig. 51. A trial trip on the Metropolitan Railway, 1863.

Fig. 52. Building at Baker Street London, 1868.

Fig. 53 (right) Tunnelling for the first sub-surface railway. Waterloo and City Underground Railway.

Fig. 54. Inside one of the first tube trains.

locomotives in others. Usually, long distance trains were brought to London under steam power, then were taken over by electric engines.

By the end of the 19th century the capital's first tube railway had been planned. It was opened in 1890 and ran from the City, first to the Elephant and Castle, then on to Stockwell. The route passed under the River Thames.

Tube railways were constructed in other parts of London. One was the famous 'Bakerloo' line which was the Baker Street and Waterloo Railway. Like the surface railways they were independent companies, striving to make a profit for their shareholders. Much of the equipment used in the early days came from the U.S.A. In the first years of the 20th century, an American, Charles T. Yerkes began to dominate the scene of London's underground system. He came to control a number of companies and introduced schemes of electrifiction.

The 'tube' became a vital part of London's transport. Every day thousands of people travelled underground to all parts of the city. The lines bored through the earth under busy roads, offices, factories and houses. The Thames could be crossed. Fares were cheap, services frequent and fast.

In 1933 the London Passenger Transport Board was formed to run the capital's transport system. The Board was nationalised in 1948. Since then, services have been expanded and a new route, the Victoria Line, has been opened. During a day there are only about four hours when trains are not running on the Underground.

Two other cities in Britain have underground railways. They are Glasgow and Liverpool. Compared with London's routes, however, their lines cover only a short distance.

Overseas, a number of other countries have

*Fig. 55. A scene on the Victoria Line, London's most
modern Underground Railway.*

built their own underground systems. Two of the world's finest are to be seen in Paris and Moscow.

Now draw a chart, in two sections, showing the development of underground railways in Britain, (a) during the 19th century, and (b) during the 20th century. Then make a list showing (a) the advantages and (b) the disadvantages, of having underground railways in a large city.

19. Narrow Gauge and Miniature Railways

Most of Britain's railway lines have been built to a gauge of 4ft 8½ins. For a period of time in the last century, the G.W.R. ran broad gauge trains at 7ft 0½ins. But there have also been a number of lines built with a narrower gauge. If the gauge is less than 2 feet, then the line is known as a miniature railway. Some of these railways ran for years before closing. Others are still in operation. Perhaps during a holiday you have been for a short journey on one of them. They are still very popular and are enjoyed as much by adults as by children.

Here is a list showing most of Britain's best known narrow gauge and miniature railways, past and present:

1. Volk's Electric Railway
2. The Vale of Rheidol Railway
3. The Corris Railway
4. The Isle of Man Railway
5. The Ravenglass and Eskdale Railway
6. The Welshpool and Llanfair Light Railway
7. The Lynton and Barnstaple Railway
8. The Festiniog Railway
9. The Manx Electric Railway
10. The Snowdon Mountain Tramroad, a rack railway
11. The Romney, Hythe and Dymchurch Light Railway
12. The Talyllyn Railway

Small locomotives can be made very successfully. There is no basic difference between them and larger engines. They need a proper boiler, firebox and smoke-box. To drive these locomotives demands a high degree of skill.

One of the most famous of small railways is the Romney, Hythe and Dymchurch Railway. It was opened in 1926 and later the line was extended to Dungeness. There are two tracks at a gauge of 15 inches. The rails are flat-bottomed, 24 lb., laid on wooden sleepers. From the start the railway has been well used. For example, in 1927 there were seven engines running. They carried, in their trains, more than a quarter of a million passengers.

The locomotives used in the 1930's were based on the *Flying Scotsman* engines of the L.N.E.R. One of them, *Typhoon* pulled a train which carried 327 passengers to Hythe from Dymchurch. The speeds usually attained were between 20 and 30 m.p.h. A

Fig. 56. The Volk's Railway at Brighton.

very good railway service has been offered to customers. During the Second World War the railway was near the front line of battle, in the south of England. It was taken over for military purposes.

Another interesting small line was the narrow gauge Lynton and Barnstaple Railway. It had a length of just over 19 miles and was laid at a gauge of 1ft 11½ins. The line ran by some of the beautiful countryside of North Devon, often along steep gradients of 1 in 50. The locomotives were tank engines, mainly Manning Wardle 2-6-2's, each weighing 22½ tons. The Southern Railway took over the line in 1923 but closed it twelve years later.

Narrow gauge lines have a great appeal to enthusiasts. They are able to see a railway working in miniature. Some have been restored and maintained with the voluntary help of preservation societies. Three are in Wales. One is the Talyllyn Railway; another is the Festiniog Railway.

The Festiniog line was built between 1832 and 1836. It was used for transporting slate, but from 1865 passengers were carried. The scenery is magnificent as it runs through the Welsh mountains, sometimes along narrow ledges. The line closed in 1946 but sections have been re-opened since 1955.

A very interesting small railway is at Brighton. It is the Volk's Electric Railway, built by Marcus Volk and opened in 1883. The gauge is 2ft 8½ins. A description of one of the early cars said that it:

. . . is a model of the interior of the deck saloon on a steam yacht; constructed of solid mahogany, plate-glass windows, a panelled ceiling with paintings of flowers and palms; blue silk curtains to the windows, mirrors and so on. The exterior is precisely that of a first-class railway carriage, with the exception that the footboards are protected by brass rails.[1]

The Volk's Railway has provided a very useful addition to Brighton's transport system. On an average it carries more than one million passengers each year.

Here are some questions:

1. *What is the difference between a narrow gauge and a miniature railway?*
2. *Why are such railways very popular in Britain?*
3. *Which narrow gauge and miniature railways still operate?*

[1]Quoted in *The Underground Story*, by H. Douglas

Fig. 57. The Romney, Hythe and Dymchurch Railway.

Fig. 58. The Festiniog Railway. The 'Earl of Merionath', July 1968.

20. Modern Stations and their Staff

In Great Britain there are thousands of railway stations. They vary enormously in size. Perhaps, while on a train journey you have stopped at a small halt where only one or two men are employed. Then at the end of the line you have come to a giant terminus, bustling with the activity of scores of porters and ticket collectors as passengers leave the train.

Every day railway stations, large and small, play a vital part in the country's system of modern transport. This occurs especially on suburban lines which feed millions of people into cities where they work. The great terminus stations work to a most detailed timetable where every minute really counts as trains are brought in, unloaded and then sent out again. The largest London terminus is Waterloo, which covers $24\frac{1}{2}$ acres, enclosing more than 20 platforms. The pace of the work there at the peak of the rush-hour is extremely hard, for over one thousand train movements are operated within 24 hours.

As well as the pressure of traffic on terminal stations there are certain junction stations which have become 'nerve centres' of Britain's railway system. The most famous and the busiest is Clapham Junction. Its 17 platforms have had more than 2000 train movements through them within one day. At peak time more than 2000 passengers pass through the station every minute.

Another famous centre is Crewe. It lies at a point where lines radiate to many parts of Britain. Tracks cross there connecting North Wales, Liverpool, Manchester, Scotland, the Potteries and various other places. Crewe became a railway town in the Victorian Age and was a centre for the operations of thousands of trains. Among other large provincial junction stations are York, Bristol and Carlisle.

At a station, the man who has the main responsibility is the station master. He controls the staff and the trains there. Such a man must be experienced in railway practice and must know in detail the work of other employees so that he understands exactly what is going on. He must also know such things as which trains detach coaches at his station or which deliver heavy parcels. If the station master is in charge of a large station he has a most complicated job which involves the taking of many important decisions.

The carrying out of much of the work at a station is performed by porters and foremen. They have to move luggage and general small freight, as well as looking after passengers.

Other staff are needed to make a station run smoothly. Booking clerks sell tickets and register the fares which are vital to keep the railways in business. Some stations employ a full time ticket collector to check tickets. Elsewhere, other members of the staff carry out the task.

In the nearby sidings, engine drivers, guards and shunters will be moving trucks and coaches round. They have to build up trains, putting rolling stock into the correct order. The work is carried out at the marshalling yards. A vital place there is the 'hump'. This is a small hill, with a single track, over which various trucks are pushed by diesel shunting engines. Once over the hump the trucks run freewheel down into the correct sidings. The points have already been set to decide which track will be used. One man can organise the building up of trains, working from a control tower.

And checking the movements of all trains are the signalmen. From their signal boxes they organise the safe running of rail traffic.

Stations have always been fascinating centres of human activity, although today they sometimes lack the colour of the past. The extract below describes the scene at a station on 1 March 1841 when the Manchester and Leeds Railway was opened:

> At a few minutes before 9.15. a.m. the clanging of the ponderous bell, which at this station is suspended in the roof, gave the signal for the carriage doors to be closed, or rather slammed. All being clear, the fanfare of the guard from aloft was quickly responded to by a piercing whistle amid the roaring steam of the engine, and the train proceeded swiftly on its way to the tuneful strains of a band, which was accommodated in one of the open carriages . . .[1]

Will there ever be a day when scientific gadgets are so advanced that a handful of men will be able to run the work of a large station, controlling the movements of scores of trains and thousands of passengers?

[1] The opening of the Manchester & Leeds Railway, 1st March 1841, source unknown

Fig. 59. Modern rush-hour traffic at Liverpool Street Station.

Fig. 60. Europe's largest marshalling yard, Kingmoor near Carlisle.

Fig. 61. A large modern station – Euston.

Can you now answer these questions?
1. *Explain these railway terms (a) control, (b) sidings, (c) booking office, (d) the 'hump'.*
2. *What are the duties of a stationmaster?*

21. Safety and Accidents

Perhaps you have been travelling in a motor car that has been moving at considerable speed when an emergency has occurred. To escape hitting an object, the driver has frantically applied the brakes and wrestled with the wheel to avoid injury to his passengers. Even on a good dry day the car may travel for 50 or 60 yards before it is finally brought to a halt.

Therefore you can imagine how much more difficult it is for a train to stop. It is far heavier than a car. Often the total weight is several hundred tons. The train will travel at a greater speed than a car. The driver cannot swerve to avoid an obstruction. The rails ensure that his course is carried forward towards the object which blocks his way. He may travel for half a mile before he can come to a halt.

Some people are alarmed by speed. In the last century one of Queen Victoria's secretaries wrote to a railway company:

> I am desired to intimate Her Majesty's wish that the speed of the Royal Train should on no account be increased at any one part of the line in order to make up for the time lost by an unforeseen delay at another . . . This order has probably arisen from one of the Directors telling Her Majesty last year that they had been driving the train at the rate of sixty miles an hour, a gratuitous piece of information which, very naturally, alarmed Her Majesty . . .[1]

A railway accident can be a major disaster. Scores of people may be killed or injured. Thousands of pounds worth of damage can be done to equipment and rolling stock. Large stretches of rail may be torn up. The effects of a railway collision can be surprising. A whole coach filled with passengers may be telescoped or hurled over an embankment or twisted to stand upright on its end. The scene after a bad crash sometimes looks as if a giant has crushed toys with hammer blows.

Yet in spite of the immense damage that an accident can cause and the enormous dangers of travelling at speed, Britain's railways are remarkably safe. Thousands of passengers travel on hundreds of journeys and arrive at their destinations without the thought of an accident. During several years of the present century, no single passenger

has been killed. There is far more likelihood of a collision on the roads than on the rails.

Since the beginning of railways in Britain there has been a great stress laid on safety. It has been a tradition that precautions should be taken to guard people carefully while they are travelling. Signalling has been developed as a fine skill. Areas of line, in blocks, are governed by signals and any traffic within them is protected. Modern signals are installed as coloured lights, which have replaced the semaphore arms of the past. The work of the signalman is vital to the running of the service and he is often directly responsible for the safety of the lives of hundreds of passengers within his section. An Automatic Warning System sends information to the driver's cab, telling him whether signals are at caution or are clear to pass.

The standards of modern safety have been achieved in many cases by the lessons learned from accidents in the past. Although few and far between, they have sometimes been very terrible and their memory lives long in railway history. Here are short accounts of three of the most remarkable accidents which have occurred in Britain. Each was different from the others in cause, but led to a heavy loss of life. At the resulting enquiries steps were taken to make railway travel safer.

The first accident occurred on the Great Eastern Railway in 1874. The movement of trains over the single line section between Thorpe and Brundall, near Norwich, was controlled by Cooke and Wheatstone telegraph linking the two stations. On 10 September, in the evening, there were two trains waiting to use the section. One was an express from Liverpool Street to Yarmouth; the other was an up Mail train.

Because of some confusion between the station staff at Thorpe, the night inspector ordered the young telegraph clerk to send a message to Brundall, calling up the Mail train. A minute later, the express drew into Thorpe and was then sent on its way by the day inspector. There had been confusion over what orders had been given; there was a fatal lack of checking the movements of the two trains.

Suddenly the station staff became aware of what

[1] A letter from the secretary to the Queen, 1850

had happened. A frantic message was telegraphed to Brundall—'Stop Mail'. But the awful reply came—'Mail left'. Nothing could be done to halt the two trains rushing towards each other through the darkness. They met at high speed in a terrible collision. Twenty-five passengers were killed and more than seventy injured.

The second accident was probably the most famous in the history of Britain's railways. It happened in 1879. In the previous year, a bridge designed by Thomas Bouch, had been opened over the River Tay in Scotland. The bridge was the world's longest at that time and appeared to be a marvellous construction. But some local people wondered how it would fare when the winter gales started to blow. The fearful answer was soon given.

A train going to Dundee stopped at the St Fort signal box at the southern end of the bridge for the driver to collect the staff which allowed him to use the single section. A gale was howling as the train rumbled on to the bridge. The signalman signalled over to the box on the other shore, 'Train entering section'. Then he, with a companion, watched the lights as the locomotive drew its carriages across the girders. Suddenly there were sparks, a flash of light, then blackness. Staggering through the gale down to the shore, the two men looked out across the raging waters. As the moon broke through they saw that the high girders, three main sections in the middle of the bridge, had gone. The pressure of the wind on the train and bridge together had been too great and 75 people had been hurled to their deaths in the foaming torrent below.

The disaster shook the railway world. At the

Fig. 62. The driver in the cab of an electric locomotive.

Fig. 63. A modern signalbox, Bletchley.

Fig. 64. (right) The scene at a railway accident. Hither Green, November 1967.

following inquiry it was shown that the bridge was far too flimsy to take the stresses which it had to stand. Bouch, the engineer, was a ruined man. In the future, more attention was paid to the planning and erection of bridges.

The last of the accidents was also the most terrible. It occurred in 1915 during the First World War, at Quintinshill, a small signal box and sidings, just to the north of Carlisle. At about 6.30 a.m. two trains were waiting, one on the up loop and one on the down loop. A third train, a local, was standing on the up main line. The two signalmen in the box were not attending thoroughly to their work and carelessly allowed a special troop train to enter the section. Running at speed it crashed into the local. The fifteen coach troop train telescoped to one third its length. The disaster was bad, but worse was to come. An express bound for Scotland now thundered on to the scene, travelling on the down line. It hurtled into the wreckage of the accident. The two trains standing on the loops were hit by flying pieces of engine and coaches. Five trains were engulfed in a massive crash. Then came an added horror. The troop train had been lit by gas, which now ignited and set fire to the wreckage. It blazed fiercely for over a day, in spite of all efforts to control it.

The death roll was the largest in British railway history. Altogether 227 people were killed, most of them soldiers of the Royal Scots. Careless and casual behaviour by the signalmen had led to a terrible disaster.

Since that time, other accidents have happened, some of them very bad. But railwaymen strive constantly to guard their passengers and eliminate human error. The aids of modern science help in this, but there are still many occasions when safety depends upon the action of individual employees. They take their responsibility very seriously.

Here are some questions:

1. *Why are there so many road accidents, yet so few railway accidents?*
2. *Read a detailed account of one of the accidents mentioned in the chapter above, then make a list of reasons why it happened.*
3. *Which modern devices help to make railway travel safe?*

22. Who Was Who and What Was What

Shown below are the names of 100 people and items of importance in the development of Britain's railway system. A few details are given about each one. You will be able to find out more about them from the books that are listed in the next chapter:

ARTICULATED LOCOMOTIVE—An engine built especially for use over difficult country. It has two independent chassis and is really two engines in one.

BALLAST—The name given to the material on which rails and sleepers are laid. It consists mainly of chipped stones.

BEECHING, DR R.—The man commissioned to produce a report on Britain's railways. When it appeared in 1963, he suggested measures to make them more efficient, including the closing of many branch lines.

BIG FOUR, THE—The name was applied to the four railway networks created after the First World War. They were the L.M.S.R., the L.N.E.R., the G.W.R. and the S.R.

BLENKINSOP, J.—A pioneer of locomotive design, he built a 'rack' locomotive in 1812.

BLOCK SYSTEM—A system of safety, controlled by signals, where in a given area no two trains may be moving on the same line of rails at the same time.

BOGIE—Small trolley wheels on which carriages or trucks are built to give easier and more comfortable movement while travelling.

BOILER—On a steam powered engine the boiler was the area where water was heated to produce the steam which drove the engine.

BOOKING OFFICE—This is the office at a station where tickets can be bought by passengers.

BRADSHAW—*Bradshaw's Guide*, first published in 1839, was a collection of the timetables of Britain's various railway companies. It helped travellers to plan their journeys.

BRASSEY, T.—A famous civil engineer who played a prominent part in the planning and construction of early railways in Britain and France.

BRITISH RAILWAYS—Later shortened to British Rail, this title was given to Britain's state owned railway system.

BRUNEL, I. K.—One of the greatest engineers of the Victorian Age, he built railways and ships. He planned the Great Western Railway and built it on the broad gauge.

BULL-HEADS—The type of rail used on Britain's railways for many years, receiving the name from its shape.

BULLEID, O. V. S.—Famous Chief Mechanical Engineer of the Southern Railway, he designed the 'Merchant Navy' class during the Second World War.

CAB—The place from which the driver controls the train. On a steam locomotive it was also called the footplate.

CHAIRS—Metal rests, fixed to the sleepers, in which the rails are held.

CHANNEL TUNNEL—At the end of the 19th century a start was made to building a tunnel under the English Channel to link Britain with France. It is proposed to go ahead with the scheme during the next few years.

CHURCHWARD, G. J.—As Chief Mechanical Engineer of the G.W.R. in the early years of the 20th century he improved the design of engines to make better use of steam.

COMMUNICATION CORD—A method by which passengers may stop the train in an emergency. The cord runs through the length of the train and is easily accessible in each compartment.

COMPOUND—A type of locomotive in which steam is used in more than one set of cylinders.

COOK, T.—As a pioneer of organising excursion trips for people during the Victorian Age, he founded the well-known travel agency.

COUPLING—This is the metal fixture which hooks and joins one truck or carriage to the next.

DEAD MAN'S HANDLE—A handle held by the driver of an electric train. When it is held down, the train can go. If it is released, then the train automatically stops.

DIESEL ENGINE—At the end of the 19th century, Rudolf Diesel, a German, invented a form of internal combustion engine. It has been developed for use on railways.

DYNAMOMETER CAR—A test coach carried on a train during tests. Its equipment records the locomotive's performance.

ELECTRIC TRACTION—Using electric power to drive a train, picking up the power either from a third rail or from overhead wires.

ESCALATOR—A moving staircase, used on underground railways for transporting passengers to and from platforms.

EXPRESS TRAIN—A fast train, stopping at few or no stations before reaching its destination.

EXCURSION—A special railway trip, often arranged to visit a particular place or event, usually at a reduced price.

FIREBOX—The part of a steam locomotive where coal was burned to heat water and produce the power to turn the engine.

FISHPLATES—Metal clips which join together two lengths of rail.

FOG SIGNALS—Small explosive charges laid on rails to warn oncoming trains in foggy conditions.

FREIGHT—The name given to goods, as opposed to passengers, carried on a railway.

GANGER—A man in charge of a group of plate-layers, responsible for the care of a length of track.

GAUGE—The distance between the two rails of a railway track. In Britain standard gauge is 4ft 8½ins.

GRADIENT—The slope of a railway line, either rising or falling.

GREATHEAD, J. H.—The inventor of the Greathead Shield, a method of boring underground and building tunnels.

GRESLEY, H. N.—A locomotive designer especially famous for his fast engines built for the L.N.E.R. in the 1930's.

HACKWORTH, T.—An engineer of early railways, he became manager of the Stockton and Darlington line.

HEDLEY, W.—An engine-wright of Wylam Colliery, he built the *Puffing Billy* in 1813.

HUDSON, G.—Known as 'The Railway King', Hudson promoted schemes for building railways in the 1840's. He made and lost a fortune.

INCLINE—A slope on which a railway line is laid.

KILLINGWORTH COLLIERY—The famous colliery in N.E. England where George Stephenson was engineer and where he pioneered some of his locomotive design.

LEVEL CROSSING—A place where a railway crosses a road and traffic is controlled by gates or barriers.

LIVERPOOL AND MANCHESTER RAILWAY—One of Britain's first railways, planned by George Stephenson and opened in 1830.

LOCOMOTIVE—The powered vehicle which draws a train along.

LONDON PASSENGER TRANSPORT BOARD—The L.P.T.B. was formed in 1933 to co-ordinate the capital's transport systems. It took over underground railways.

MAIL TRAIN—From their early days, trains replaced horse-drawn coaches as carriers of the Royal Mail. Some trains are specially equipped for carrying postal services.

MARSHALLING YARDS—Areas of track, away from main lines, where trucks and coaches can be shunted and arranged as trains.

METROPOLITAN RAILWAY—The World's first sub-surface railway, opened in London in 1863.

MONORAIL—An overhead single rail from which a train can be suspended to travel at high speed.

NAVVIES—The name given to the construction workers who built the early railways during the 19th century.

NATIONALISATION—Ownership by the State as opposed to ownership by private individuals or companies.

NEWCOMEN, T.—Thomas Newcomen invented a number of atmospheric engines, powered by steam, between 1705 and 1712.

PANTOGRAPH—An attachment which connects an electric train to overhead wires and draws the power to the engine.

PARLIAMENTARY TRAINS—The Cheap Trains Act of 1844 stipulated that railway companies should run cheap services for working class people. They were nicknamed 'Parliamentary Trains'.

PEARSON, C.—A Member of Parliament who pioneered a scheme to give London its first underground railway.

PERMANENT WAY—The name given to the track of a railway.

PLATFORM—The part of a station from which passengers can board or leave trains.

POINTS—The part of a railway where two sets of lines meet and trains can be transferred from one track to another.

PULLMAN COACHES—Luxury coaches in which passengers can obtain meals and refreshments while travelling.

PUSH-AND-PULL—A small train, often used on a single-line track, where the engine does not change ends, but pushes in one direction and pulls in the other.

QUINTINSHILL—The scene of Britain's greatest ever rail disaster in 1915. Five trains were involved and 227 people were killed.

RACK LOCOMOTIVE—A form of locomotive in which cogs on the wheels fitted into notches at the side of the rails in order to give a better grip.

RAILWAY CLEARING HOUSE—An organisation

set up in 1842 to organise the sharing of receipts from passengers and freight travel.

RAILWAY MANIA—The name given to the vast speculation in railway building which took place from 1845–1846.

RAILWAYS AMALGAMATION ACT—Passed in 1921, the Act came into operation in 1923. It re-organised Britain's railways into four companies.

RAINHILL TRIALS—Held in 1829 at Rainhill, near Manchester, the trials were a test to find a suitable locomotive for the Liverpool and Manchester Railway.

'ROCKET', THE—George Stephenson's famous locomotive, built for the Rainhill Trials. At present it is in the Science Museum.

ROLLING STOCK—The name given to trucks and carriages belonging to a railway company.

SAVERY, T.—A pioneer of steam pumping engines at the end of the 17th century.

SEASON TICKET—A ticket bought by travellers who make regular journeys over a certain route, usable for a period of time.

SIGNAL—A method of transmitting information to train crews. Semaphore arms were once used, but now they have been replaced by coloured lights.

SINGLES—Locomotives, built in the 19th century, having one pair of driving wheels.

SLEEPER—A wooden or concrete rest on which rails are mounted. It is similar to a thick plank.

STEAM ENGINE—An engine using steam from boiling water to obtain its power.

STEPHENSON, G.—George Stephenson, the 'Father of English Railways', a truly great engineer of loco-motive and railway construction.

STEPHENSON, R.—Robert Stephenson, the son of George, was also a famous railway engineer.

STIRLING, P.—Engineer of the Great Northern Railway, he built a number of famous 'singles' with large driving wheels.

STOCKTON AND DARLINGTON RAILWAY—Britain's first railway, opened in 1825. Originally intended for carrying coal, it also transported passengers.

STROUDLEY, W.—An engineer of the London, Brighton and South Coast Railway in the 19th century.

STREAMLINING—The designing of locomotives so that wind resistance is lessened and greater speeds obtained.

SURREY IRON RAILWAY—One of Britain's first railway lines, it was used by horse-drawn trucks from 1803.

TANK ENGINE—A locomotive without a separate tender, carrying its supply of coal and water at the rear of its frame.

TAY BRIDGE DISASTER—A terrible accident which occurred in 1879 when the bridge collapsed as a train was crossing it.

TELEGRAPH—A method of sending signals or messages to different parts of the railway system, usually to warn of the approach or departure of a train.

TENDER—A type of truck carried immediately behind a steam locomotive and intended for hold-ing water and coal.

TIMETABLE—The published list of arrival and de-parture times of a company's trains, useful for passengers and essential for safety.

TRAMWAYS—The old name given to a line of wooden rails laid in colliery areas.

TREVITHICK, R.—A great pioneer of steam loco-motion. He experimented with vehicles for road and rail transport in the late 18th and early 19th centuries.

TUBE—The name given to London's first under-ground railway which was opened in 1890.

UNDERGROUND—The name given to the Metro-politan Railway, which was the world's first sub-surface line.

VACUUM—A space without any air. Vacuum brakes were devised to work when air was let into a tube.

VIADUCT—A railway viaduct is a bridge which carries the line over a valley or road or river.

WATER TROUGH—The water trough lay between the rails. When travelling at speed the driver of a steam locomotive could lower a gadget to scoop up water, thereby replenishing his supply without stopping the train.

WATT, J.—James Watt, one of history's great engineering geniuses, introduced rotary motion into the action of the steam engine, enabling it to be developed for use in transport.

WEBB, F. W.—A pioneer of compound engines, he was Locomotive Superintendent of the London and North Western Railway from 1871 to 1903.

WESTINGHOUSE BRAKE—The compressed air brake devised by an American, George Westing-house, in 1869, brought greater safety to rail travel.

YERKES, C. T.—An American who came to own a number of companies of underground railways in London, bringing in schemes of electrification.

The Time Line opposite gives some of the most important dates in the story of the railways of Britain. Can you find any other events of note which occurred in those years?

1784	Murdoch's steam driven vehicle	1863	Opening of the first underground railway
1803	The Surrey Iron Railway		
1808	Trevithick's 'Catch-me-who-can' in London	1869	Westinghouse brake invented
1812	Blenkinsop's rack locomotive	1873	Introduction of sleeping carriages
1825	The Stockton and Darlington Railway	1874	Introduction of Pullman carriages
1829	The Rainhill Trials	1879	Tay Bridge Disaster
1830	The Liverpool and Manchester Railway	1895	The Railway Races
		1921	Railways Amalgamation Act
1839	First Bradshaw published	1933	Formation of L.P.T.B.
1842	Railway Clearing House established	1948	Nationalization of Britain's railways
1845–6	'Railway Mania'		
1851	The Great Exhibition		
1856	Invention of the Bessemer process		

Now complete the Time Line for the years since 1948, adding the dates and events which you consider to have been important.

23. Further Study

This book has been written particularly as a starting point for people who wish to make a study of the history of railways. It is only an introduction. If you wish to learn more about this interesting subject here are some suggestions and hints.

You may want to write your own account as a topic in a folder or book. This may be a piece of examination work or it may be done for your own interest. There are certain ways to approach the work in order to study it thoroughly.

1. Plan out your work. Write an outline showing the number of chapters. Do not try to study too much. Do you wish to study the whole history of railways or just one aspect of it?
2. Gather up your information. Read a wide variety of newspapers, magazines and books. Collect photographs and printed information. Make drawings and tracings. Visit museums and write to find what exhibits they have. Talk with older people who have had experience in the world of railways.
3. First write out your work in rough. Make your mistakes there, not in your final copy. THINK FIRST, THEN WRITE, THEN CHECK. Check your rough work several times.
4. Write or type out your final copy.
5. Make sure that it is written out in your own words. Gather your information from as many sources as possible, but make sure that it is presented in your own words and not copied wholesale from a book.
6. A reader should be able to learn a lot from your work. The facts must be carefully checked. Do not give opinions unless you understand them well.
7. The arrangement of your work will count for a great deal. Make sure that your handwriting is neat or your typing set out carefully. Photographs and other illustrations need to be arranged attractively.
8. Give a list of the contents of your study at the front. At the back, mention your sources of information.

This book mentions a number of ways in which you may obtain further information and material.

First, there are weekly and monthly publications which may be bought or ordered at any newsagent's shop. They are usually reasonable in price and contain not only information but also addresses from which you may discover further knowledge.

Second, here is a list of one hundred books which deal with the story of railways. Search for them at your local library. If the library does not have them, the librarian will be able to obtain them for you. You may wish to buy some of the books yourself.

There have been many books published on aspects of this subject. Those shown here vary in difficulty. Use as many as you can to gain different information and viewpoints.

Adams, J. & Whitehouse, P. B., *Railway Picture Gallery*
Allen, C. J., *British Railways for Boys*
Allen, C. J., *Modern Railways*
Allen, C. J., *The Romantic Story of the Iron Road*
Allen, G. C., *Railways*
Ashmore, O., *Development of Power in Britain*
Bagwell, P. S., *The Railwaymen*
Barker, T. C. & Robbins, M., *A History of London Transport*
Barman, C. *Early British Railways*
Barnes, E. G., *The Rise of the Midland Railways, 1844–1874*
Beal, E., *Modelling the Old Time Railways*
Behrend, G., *Grand European Expresses*
Blower, A., *British Railway Tunnels*
Boulton, W. H., *The Railways of Britain*
Bryant, E. T., *Railways*
Bulleid, H. A. V., *Master Builders of Steam*
Calvert, R., *The Future of Britain's Railways*
Carter, E. F., *Britain's Railway Liveries*
Carter, E. F., *Let's Look at Trains*
Carter, E. F., *Railways in Wartime*
Carter, E. F., *The Boy's Book of World Railways*
Carter, E. F., *The True Book about Railways*
Cox, E. S., *Locomotive Panorama*
Darwin, B., *War on the Line*
Davies, W. J. K., *Light Railways*
Day, J. R., *More Unusual Railways*
Day, J. R., *Railways Under the Ground*
Day-Lewis, S., *Bulleid: Last Giant of Steam*
Derry, T. K. & Williams, T. I., *A Short History of Technology*

Dickinson, H. W., *A Short History of the Steam Engine*
Douglas, H., *The Underground Story*
Elton, A., *British Railways*
Foxwell, E. & Farrer, T. C., *Express Trains, English and Foreign*
Fry, L., *British Railways*
Fry, L., *Railways*
Garnett, E., *The Master Engineers*
Garnett, E., *The Railway Builders*
Gifford, C. T., *Decline of Steam*
Gordon, W. J., *Our Home Railways*
Greenwood, M., *Railway Revolution, 1825–1845*
Halson, G. R., *Discovering Railways*
Hamilton, J. A. B., *Britain's Railways in World War I*
Hamilton-Ellis, C., *British Railway History*
Hamilton-Ellis, C., *A Picture History of Railways*
Havers, H. C. P., *Underground Railways of the World*
Hennessey, R. A. S., *Transport*
Hogg, G., *Union Pacific*
Holcroft, H., *Locomotive Adventure*
Horsley Denton, J., *British Railway Stations*
Jackman, W. T., *Development of Transportation in Modern England*
Jackson, A. A., *Volk's Railway, Brighton, 1883–1964*
Jackson, A. A. & Croome, D. F., *Rails Through the Clay*
Johns, C., *The Picture Story of World Railways*
Kidner, R. W., *The London, Chatham & Dover Railway*
Kinchenside, G. M., *Railway Carriage Album*
Kinchenside, G. M., *Railway Carriages, 1839–1939*
Law, R. J., *The Steam Engine*
Lloyd, R., *Railwayman's Gallery*
Longacre Book of Trains
Loxton, H., *Railways*
McDermot, E. J., *The History of the Great Western Railway*
Meynell, L., *Builder and Dreamer*
Morgan, B. (edt.), *The Railway Lover's Companion*
Nock, O. S., *British Steam Locomotives at Work*
Nock, O. S., *The Railway Engineers*
Nock, O. S., *The Railways of Britain, past and present*
Ottley, E., *Bibliography of Railway History*
Oxford Junior Encyclopaedia, vol. IV, Communications
Oxford University Press, *A History of Technology*, 5 vols.
Passingham, W. J., *The Romance of London's Underground*

Prebble, J., *The High Girders*
Ransome-Wallis, P., *British Railways Today*
Ransome-Wallis, P., *The Concise Encyclopaedia of World Railway Locomotives*
Ray, J. P., *The History of Transport in Britain, 1700 to the present*
Redmayne, P., *Transport by Land*
Robbins, M., *The Railway Age*
Rogers, H. C. B., *Turnpike to Iron Road*
Rolt, L. T. C., *George and Robert Stephenson*
Rolt, L. T. C., *Red for Danger*
Sherrington, C., *A Hundred Years of Inland Transport, 1830–1933*
Simon, H. & Fenton, W., *About Railways*
Simmons, J., *The Railways of Britain*
Simmons, J., *Transport*
Simmons, T. H., *Railways to the end of the Nineteenth Century*
Snell, J. B., *Early Railways*
Snell, J. B., *The Book of Trains*
Snellgrove, L. E., *From 'Rocket' to Railcar*
Stover, J. S., *American Railroads*
Taylor, M., *Going by Train*
Thomas, J., *The Story of George Stephenson*
Thornhill, P., *Railways for Britain*
Tomlinson, W. W., *The North Eastern Railway*
Vallance, H. A. (edt.), *The Railway Enthusiast's Bedside Book*
Way, R. B., *The Story of British Locomotives*
Wescott, G. F., *The British Railway Locomotive, 1803–1853*
Wescott Jones, K., *Great Railway Journeys of the World*
Whitbread, J. R., *The Railway Policeman*
Whitehouse, P. B., *Steam in Europe*
Whitehouse, P. B., *Branch Line Album*

There are in Great Britain a number of collections and museums which show various aspects of the history of railways. To visit them is very rewarding. Have you seen any of them yet? And do you know of any other places where such collections are kept?

1. The Museum of British Transport, Clapham, London.
2. The Railway Museum, York.
3. The Science Museum, South Kensington, London.
4. The Great Western Railway Museum, Swindon, Wiltshire.

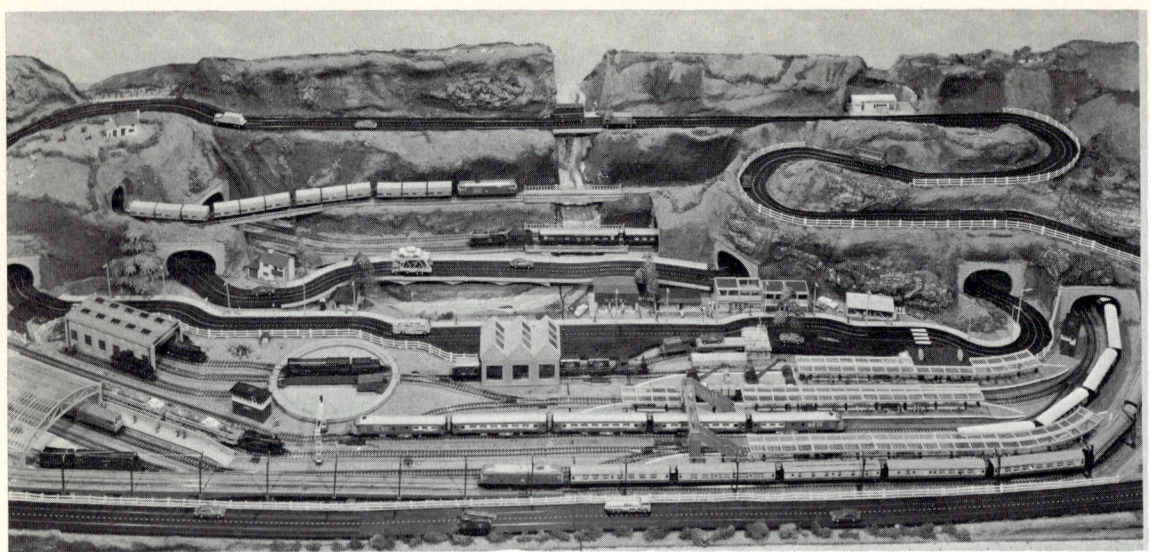

Fig. 65. A model railway display.   *Fig. 66. (right) Exhibits at the Science Museum.*

For photographic material, there are a number of agencies. Some provide illustrations free of charge. Usually, they are the public relations departments of commercial companies connected with transport by rail. Others provide photographs for a fee. They include:

1. The Radio Times Hulton Picture Library, 35 Marylebone High Street, London, W.1.
2. The Science Museum, South Kensington, London.

24. Questions

The following chapter consists of questions about railways. By finding the answers you will improve your knowledge of the subject:

1. When:

(a) Was the Railways Amalgamation Act passed?
(b) Was the Stockton and Darlington Railway opened?
(c) Was the Metropolitan Railway opened?
(d) Was the Beeching Report produced?

2. Where:

(a) Is Britain's largest station?
(b) Is Waverley Station?
(c) Is Killingworth Colliery?
(d) Is the highest line in the World?
(e) Is the Kilsby Tunnel?

3. Who:

(a) Were the navvies?
(b) Designed the *Mallard*?
(c) Was the first engineer of the G.W.R?
(d) Built a line across Chat Moss?
(e) Was 'the Railway King'?

4. Which:

(a) Other forms of transport were affected by the early railways?
(b) Company had most electric trains before 1939?
(c) Inventor built a steel converter in 1856?
(d) British company first used Pullman cars?
(e) Railway built the world's largest steam locomotives?

5. What:

(a) Are bogie wheels?
(b) Is standard gauge?
(c) Is a flat-bottomed rail?
(d) Was the engine's sand-box?
(e) Are marshalling yards?

6. Match the following pairs together correctly:

(a) Excursions	(a) Bradshaw
(b) George Stephenson	(b) Clapham
(c) Brakes	(c) *Catch-me-who-can*
(d) T. Edmondson	(d) L.B. & S.C.R.
(e) Accident	(e) *Novelty*
(f) R. Trevithick	(f) *Blücher*
(g) Junction	(g) Tickets
(h) Timetables	(h) G. Westinghouse
(i) *Southern Belle*	(i) Thorpe
(j) The Rainhill Trials	(j) T. Cook

7. Arrange the following in the order in which they happened:

(a) The Surrey Iron Railway opened
(b) The 'Railway Races'
(c) Invention of the link-motion gear
(d) Hedley's *Puffing Billy*
(e) The evacuation from Dunkirk
(f) James Watt's double-acting steam engine
(g) The last steam journey on British Rail
(h) 'Railway Mania'
(i) Opening of the Simplon No. 2 Tunnel
(j) Founding of the Great Eastern Railway

8. Which one is out of place in each group of these?

1. (a) Midland Railway   (c) Caledonian Railway
   (b) Great Eastern Railway   (d) London and North Eastern Railway

2. (a) *Golden Arrow*   (c) *Caerphilly Castle*
   (b) *Flying Scotsman*   (d) *Cheltenham Flyer*

3. (a) Wainwright   (c) Webb
   (b) Bessemer   (d) Gooch

4. (a) Box   (c) Forth
   (b) Severn   (d) Sevenoaks

5. (a) guard   (c) fireman
   (b) driver   (d) foreman

9. *Write one or two paragraphs on the following subjects:*

    (a) Railways in Ireland
    (b) Docks and port installations owned by British Railways
    (c) How a diesel locomotive works
    (d) Railway speed records
    (e) Model railways

10. *Write at greater length—20–30 minutes each—on these topics:*

    (a) Outline the life and work of George Stephenson.
    (b) What were the effects of the railway on life in Victorian Britain?
    (c) Show how Britain's railways have met with increasing competition from other forms of transport in the 20th century.
    (d) Is there any future for Britain's railways?

Index